An Adventure

Where the Wind Wills

D. Flower

Author's Note:

To write this book, I relied upon my personal journals, researched facts, consulted with the people who appear in the book when I could, and called upon my own recollections of the events and conversations that appear throughout this memoir.

I have changed the names of most of the individuals and modified identifying details to preserve anonymity. I occasionally omitted people and events, but only when that omission had no impact on either the veracity or the substance of the narrative.

Quote Page

*L*et the wind blow and sing its songs to stir the emotions, let it bring the sweet memories of times gone and hopes for a good future ahead. Let the wind remind us that we are here in this present moment, in the gift of living, and call us to adore those whom are close and give their days to us. Let the wind rustle in the trees and sway the grassy wands, moving the fur of a mouse and the hair of a king all the same. Let the wind come as a wall, only to open up and allow us passage through, curling around us if it were a soft quilt all along. Let the wind speak of adventures and rouse the noble heart into the ways of the hero whom is strong for others and willing to take on the unsurety that comes with helping others. For the wind is all this, confident and flexible, changeable and free.

**—Angela Abraham,
author and founder of Descriptionari**

Part I

CHANGE IS IN THE AIR

Whatever you can do or dream you can, begin it!
Boldness has genius, power and magic in it.
Begin it now!

—John Anster's translation of Faust

In the Eye of the Storm

All journeys have secret destinations
of which the traveler is unaware.

—Martin Buber

Summer 2005
Omo River, Ethiopia

I arrive in Ethiopia knowing that this is not a trip for the faint of heart. I know this based on a disclaimer I'm required to sign: *One must have a willingness to endure physical hardships and ethical challenges in a harsh and remote area of Africa.* Steve Turner, owner of Origins Safaris, invited me on this trip for the purpose of documenting a Samburu Circumcision Ceremony that will be taking place on the full moon in Kenya. We've journeyed off the beaten path into Ethiopia as we await the moon's fullness. This is the bravest thing I have ever done on my own.

Suffering from exhaustion after successfully orchestrating a major event as an interpretive park ranger, and emotional after leaving a three-year relationship, I'm looking for a place of solace where I can connect to people still in touch with their ancient culture. To achieve this, I am willing to go to the other side of the world and reside in a small six-tent camp on the banks of a remote waterway. Fewer than sixty guests per year arrive at this destination.

The Great Rift Valley splits Ethiopia into nearly two equal parts, running in a ragged diagonal from the wastelands of the Danakil Depression in the northeast to the crocodile haunts of Lake Turkana in the southwest. In 1980, UNESCO declared the Lower Omo Valley a World Heritage Site in recognition of its uniqueness and the significance of the Omo tribes. Sixteen tribes inhabit this river valley, an area the size of New Hampshire. Paleontologists have discovered the remnants of our shared heritage: the oldest remains of modern humans. Archeological evidence places our oldest human ancestors in Ethiopia's Omo River Valley approximately 195,000 years ago.

Some say, 'Mitochondrial Eve,' the woman from whom all modern humans descended, lived in this part of Africa. She never migrated, but several millennia later her progeny did. This area is a land of few roads and no bridges. The river runs its course in approximately five hundred miles winding through gorges of volcanic rock and channels of ancient mud. Anthropological findings in Tanzania and Turkana, Kenya, date back as much as three and four million years ago.

I'm glad I've joined Steve for this adventure. Steve, who's more like an Australian of the "no worries" variety, thrives on this type of safari. He's willing to take six enthusiasts with him: Larry and Stan, photographers from the US, who I find to be friendly and mild-mannered; Bill, a photographer from the UK, who's comical and keeps me laughing throughout the trip; Bob, a photographer from Australia, who's demanding at times but shows a great deal of respect for women; and Elizabeth, a U.S. college professor, who's writing an essay on the sexual mores of the tribes.

After taking a charter bush plane from Nairobi to the northeastern end of Lake Turkana, we're driven in a customized Land Cruiser for three hours over rough terrain to Omorate, a town in Ethiopia near the Kenyan border. Here we will present our visas to the authorities. A faded poster on the back wall of the official, one-room administrative center says, "Coffee. Ethiopia's Gift to the World." We all agree.

Continuing off the main road, jouncing along a muddy track, we eventually meet up and board the Omo's only motorized boat. This sixteen-foot, aluminum flat-bottom style boat is piloted by Thaddeus, a Nord, who's been living and operating a meager resort on the eastern side of Lake Turkana for the past ten years.

In the next eight days, we will motor up a swift current from our tent camp to encounter the tribal villages of the Karo, Mursi, Hamar, Daasanech, and Nyangatom. Ethiopians are justifiably proud of their range of traditions, hairstyles, costumes, and heritage. Young men and women use paint made from powered white limestone as an insecticide and to turn their entire bodies into abstract canvases. Karo men boast plaited hair. Hamar women decorate themselves with colorful beaded necklaces and strings of white cowrie shells to ensure fertility; warriors display elaborate scarification on their chests and backs to signify kills of animals or enemies. Some tribes create scars in geometric patterns for pure decoration, to relieve maladies, or to teach their young the endurance of pain as a testament to their bravery.

Most women dress in goatskins worn loosely around their well-oiled bodies. Others sport coiled metal bracelets and seashell necklaces. Male and female circumcision is practiced in all but one of the tribes. The most distressing occurrence is hearing rumors of infanticide of babies stigmatized as *mingi*. A child born out of wedlock or a child with a disability fits this description. Allegedly, they may be killed because of the bad luck they are believed to bring to the tribe. Even though this is shocking, I still have a huge amount of respect for the people here since they are living and surviving in some of the harshest conditions in the world.

The tribes have the purest form of democracy: decisions must be made unanimously before anything can proceed. We're frequently delayed waiting for confirmation by the tribal elders, all men, about whether we may enter a village or take a photograph.

In one small village, I begin to photograph a father with a small child. All seems to be fine, but unexpectedly a man with a gun jumps up, shouts, and begins to approach me. None of us can understand the words, but we recognize the body language, the tone of voice, and the implications. We quickly return to our boat and continue up river without further incident.

Cattle and goats represent wealth, but so do guns. Tribal members can buy a semi-automatic weapon for $250 or twenty-five cows. I find this alarming. In the South there is a tradition of tribal conflict, and in the remote areas, the young warriors carry guns rather than spears. Even though tribal wars and revenge killings seem to be the norm, so does a sense of family, love of music and dance, demonstrations of joy or sadness, and the love of beauty. Most of the people we encounter have a genuine interest in us, in particular, the color of our skin, the texture of our hair, and the uniqueness of our belongings such as sunglasses, water bottles, cameras, and clothing. We have a reciprocal interest in why they have self-inflicted scars on their bodies and concern for the pain they must endure; their animal skins worn for clothing; the elaborate hairstyles that must take hours to complete; the uniqueness of their adornments such as neck, arm, and ankle rings that are so tight they appear to be limiting circulation; and the nails driven through some women's lower lips.

This evening we hear gunfire in the middle of the night and find out in the morning a young man has been shot. "Hopefully, just an accident," I say. But we are told they kill each other for various reasons like jealousy, envy, revenge, or just because they believe they've been insulted. It remains unsettling for me regardless.

Omo River tribal members walk weekly to the Hamar Market in Dimeka. For many, it's a three-day trek. For us, as we leave the river today and travel by safari vehicle, it's a three-hour drive. Items for sale are fish, vegetables, salt, cloth, and livestock, but we're here to meet the people. Some of my favorite interactions are with the Hamar women. These women live in a mountainous region of the eastern Lower Omo Valley and farm as well as raise goats, sheep, and cows. They barter their surplus produce and livestock at these weekly markets in Dimeka and Turmi. They are also honey-gatherers and fine potters. Many women cover their hair with a mixture of red-ocher coloring and animal fat, then style it in plaits over their foreheads. Leather and metal neck rings, which are never removed, signify a woman's marital status. An engaged woman wears one ring, a married woman two. Goatskin skirts are designed to be longer in the back than the front and resemble the tail of a gazelle.

I learn that when young men are bull jumping, their female sisters are going through a whipping ceremony. They provide an elder with a green stick and ask to be whipped on the back so hard the action draws blood. To the Hamar girls, the scars they receive from these whippings are beautiful and something that gives them a sense of pride.

Elizabeth and I roam the mud-packed street together. When I see a dilapidated pool table sitting outside by a street vendor, my competitive nature kicks in. I join some young men in a game that's already in progress. We also enjoy interacting with the children, who are allowed to tumble and play without reprimand. Teenage girls are attracted to us like magnets and follow us everywhere. I let a sweet young girl wear my sunglasses. She and her friends giggle when I show them the photographs I have taken.

The guys on our trip enjoy flirting with the young tribal women, some of whom are topless. Then when a young Hamar man begins to flirt with me, the guys seem upset. He wants my shirt, my hat, and my sunglasses. He keeps pointing to the sun and acting as if he's suffering from heat stroke and then we both laugh. Next, he wants my water bottle.

I hold it close and say, "Mine," even though I would give him anything he desires in other circumstances since he's so very handsome. I stretch my arms out to signify the length of the river that is his water source. We have an understanding of sorts, but he continues to stay by my side. With his backwards ball cap, his cool swagger, and friendly demeanor, he looks like a rap star on safari. When I meet up with Stan and Larry, they chide me, "He didn't just want your water bottle. He wanted *you.*"

One young woman I meet along the dirt path smiles at me as I point to my camera, and she shakes her head. Her hair is slick with animal fat and bright red mud woven into short braids. She carries a bundle of wood on her back and has a young child at her side. Her eyes are piercing but soft and soulful. We have a moment of primal connection. I snap a photo and then can't get her out of my mind. I would love to return someday to show her the photograph that's going to end up on the cover of *Legacy* magazine.

A wedding ceremony is taking place tonight. We observe the preparations. Already the children are dancing: young boys, naked except for beaded necklaces and young girls wearing animal-skin skirts. The smell of roasted goat entices us to stay, but darkness has already descended, and we have to drive the three hours back to Lumale Camp for the night. Within a mile before we officially arrive, we can see smoke rising over the river carrying with it the aroma of grilled beef, our dinner.

Most tribes have villages along the river for survival and trade, but due to a skirmish a few days earlier, the Mursi were driven inland by one of their enemies. We advocate for our brand of democracy, majority rule, and take a vote to decide if we want to try and follow them since they are the only people along our route who wear lip plates. This means abandoning the boat for a truck and pursuing them on a fourteen-hour expedition. The vote count is four in favor and two opposed. Of course, I'm in favor.

My stomach is upset the morning of our departure and I'm not sure whether I should join the group or stay in camp. I search through my backpack and find a small packet of instant oatmeal, comfort food I brought from home for such occasions. Adding warm water, I slurp it up and decide to climb on board as the truck is departing.

After jostling over rough terrain up and down mountain roads for eight hours with clouds of dust inundating our lungs, covering our mouths, and burning our eyes, McDonald, our driver, yells, "Tsetse flies!"

The tsetse fly is a blood feeding carrier of microscopic parasites that transfer to the host's bloodstream. Once inside, these parasites breach the immune system by constantly changing their antigenic character through massive reproduction, which causes 'sleeping sickness' in human and domestic cattle. No humans or cattle can survive in their mist.

Our invaders come in like dive bombers, biting my neck, hands, and face. Hordes enter through the floor vents zooming up my pants stinging my legs. They stay with us for over a mile. Australian Bob's face has been bitten so brutally and is so red and swollen that he no longer resembles himself when we finally encounter the Mursi.

The first Western travelers to make contact with the Mursi assumed that elaborately decorated clay lip plates worn by the young women were used to render tribal women unattractive to slavers. We find out that they are actually worn by women as a sign of entering adulthood and they signify her bride price. The larger the lip plate the higher the bride price hence her family's wealth and status. Today the young woman with the largest lip plate, seven inches in diameter, removes it from her mouth and hands it to me. A feeling of reluctance overcomes me, but ultimately, I'm excited to receive such a wonderful gift. This simple act between women from different cultures acknowledging each other's humanity cannot be described in words.

On our last day in the Omo River Valley, the sound of water lapping against the mud bank of the river gently awakens me. It takes me a minute to realize where I am. The early morning is hard to distinguish from the night.

After struggling to open the tent flap, I step out into the fresh air. Three women from the Karo tribe are below me on the steep bank already washing clothes and collecting drinking water for the day. Three empty dugout canoes float nearby, stirring the brown liquid slightly, and at first glance, I mistake them for the Nile crocodiles that infest this river. Pit stops along the banks for the past several days have caused me to have these bizarre kinds of hallucinations.

I wait my turn at the make-shift shower to pull the string that will release a bucket of river water over my head to prepare my body for the heat of the day and our boat trip down to the Omo Delta and into the desert sea called Lake Turkana. According to *National Geographic*, Lake Turkana is the world's largest permanent desert lake and has existed in this region for some four million years, expanding and contracting in a volcanic trough along the edge of the Great Rift Valley. Algae growth in pools at Lake Turkana's southern edge led early explorers to dub it the Jade Sea.

Lake Turkana holds the world's largest crocodile colony. In the 1960s biologists estimated it had fourteen thousand Nile crocs alone, but little research on their numbers has been done since. A crocodile's stealthy approach, barely detectable, can suddenly erupt into an explosion of energy, turning the water into a boil as it clamps it jaws on an unsuspecting victim. Yet the Turkana remain amazingly casual about the danger from these reptiles in spite of the number of people killed or maimed by crocodiles each year, which over time has become legendary.

Meanwhile, the traditional ritual of making Ethiopian coffee is taking place even in this remote place. I can already smell the fine beans roasting as the aroma wafts through the sparse trees that surround the camp. After a breakfast of English biscuits and jam, Steve instructs us to pack our belongings. My Patagonia backpack takes less than five minutes to load.

With time on my hands, I walk into the forested area. I see a little person peeking from behind the trees. We play this game of peek-a-boo for a few moments. It's my new Karo friend, ten-year-old Mito, who runs up beside me. He is limping. He shows me the cuts on the bottom of his feet. This concerns me. We walk slowly and quietly. He befriended me eight days ago when our group arrived at this camp. He was my shadow until I decided to walk up to the place called the Ceremonial House. It reminded me of the Parthenon in Greece that was duplicated in Nashville, Tennessee, as a part of the Centennial Exposition in 1897. Halfway up the knoll, Mito ran off when he spotted the tribal elders congregating at the summit.

Our local interpreter, McDonald, asked me, "Where are you going?"

"I want to see this place made out of twigs and logs." I reply.

"This is a man's place," he says, "where Karo tribal elders receive tributes of sorghum beer and discuss important issues. No women or children are welcome." Nevertheless, he consults with the chief.

What a surprise. I'm given permission not only to walk around the structure but to photograph the tribal elders as well. McDonald, our interpreter; Steve, our guide; and Thaddeus, our boat captain, are astonished. They've never witnessed a woman gain access to this sacred place.

While I've been exploring the Ceremonial House, Mito has been waiting for me at the bottom of the hill. He points to the forested area, and I focus through the trees. A group of men are seated in a circle in a clearing. I'm surprised to see Thaddeus sitting amongst them. He looks oddly out of place with his Nordic pale complexion, large muscular frame, and blond hair. He has endeared himself to the tribes on the Omo River by participating in their ceremonies, especially the bull jumping, that young men perform as a rite of passage. Before a man can marry, he must leap naked across the backs of lined-up cattle four times without falling. Rumor has it that Thaddeus was successful at this and the tribe presented him with a young Karo woman as his bride. I strain to see if Thaddeus has a notch in his ear, the tribal way of showing that he has completed the bull-jumping ritual and is now considered to be an elder of the tribe. I suspect he does but it isn't visible from my vantage point.

Suddenly, a tall man approaches us. He sports a bright-green feather headdress and holds his wooden stool as is customary among the men here. I feel uneasy and can only assume this is Mito's father. Maybe he has seen me slipping some money into Mito's hand. He looks into my eyes, offers his hand, and we greet.

I hug Mito and say, "My friend."

Then I show him what's in his son's hand. I point to my shoes and then to Mito's bare feet, hoping he understands that I'm providing assistance for his son to buy shoes at the market to protect his feet. I give a nod. He reciprocates, takes leave, and returns to the council meeting.

As I head back to camp, I can hear my travel mates joking around. No one appears to have their bags packed. Australian Bob is making sure he will have Tusker beer on the boat for the day. Larry is taking photographs to be used in his upcoming coffee table book. Stan is playing with his GPS, attempting to set a reading to map our trip. Bill is negotiating with a young Karo man for a beaded headband. And Elizabeth, the only other woman on the trip, is removing her bra and handing it to a young Karo girl. Steve catches my eye, and we smile. He ambles towards me and shares some celebrity gossip that he has just heard over the two-way radio: Angelina Jolie is in Ethiopia adopting a baby girl. *Interesting.*

When Thaddeus rejoins us, he makes it clear that everyone needs to be ready to depart at nine before the prevailing winds have a chance to build into an impending storm.

Am I the only one who senses how stressed Thaddeus is with our tardiness in preparing to get underway?

Even so I'm not ready to leave the Omo River. I would like to stay on with Thaddeus at the resort, but that's not possible now. Our schedule for the past week has been to leave the river during the daylight hours and visit the tribes that live high on its cliffs and to camp on its banks at night. This morning we will follow the river south to where it flows into Lake Turkana, formerly named Lake Rudolf, after the Hapsburg Crown Prince Rudolf of Austria in 1888, by Count Samuel Teleki de Szek, one of the first white explorers to travel into this sparsely inhabited part of Africa. The Samburu originally called this lake Basso Narok, meaning Black Lake, and it wasn't called Lake Turkana until Jomo Kenyatta, the first president of Kenya, changed its name in 1975.

As we finally load the flat-bottom boat, I lag behind, noticing that Bill is trying to negotiate with a young Karo man for a beautiful beaded headband. When Bill walks away dejected, I approach the young man, hand over the small amount of money I have left, and a smile erupts on his face, then mine. When I enter the boat sporting the headband, Bill is visibly upset. Laughter erupts. I must admit I'm amused.

Bill promises, "I will send you my latest coffee table book if you will give me the headband." I do, and he places it on his safari hat. All is well in the world.

The villagers are singing a song of farewell as Mito runs along the bluff past the cluster of huts, goat pens, and

stick-and-grass granary shelters, waving as we get underway. Even though we have missed our recommended departure time by one hour, we, the neophytes, anticipate a
calm sea. I extend my hand over the side of the boat to feel
the warmth of the Omo River for the last time.

The trip is estimated to take two hours. Our first hour
goes by smoothly. I sit relaxed, the warmth of the morning
sun against my body giving me an overwhelming feeling of
contentment. We ease down the river past herders wield-
ing long poles to guide their goats along the banks. The
dark river water will soon shift from charcoal to azure to
jade as we move through the delta into the lake. I'm deep in
thought, making mental footnotes of the past eight days.
When I turn and gaze back at the peaceful delta, I can still
make out the shapes of one of its residents, large white
pelicans.

Then without warning, the wind rises, whipping the
lake into a storm within minutes. Huge waves materialize
out of serene waters. The spray created by the high seas hits
me in the face and I taste the saltwater splashing into my
mouth. Our small vessel is being tossed about with gale-
force winds. High waves are sweeping over the bow soaking
me entirely. We dip and bob like a small buoy in the middle
of this turquoise sea.

Thaddeus knew that sudden and ferocious katabatic
winds could funnel down the lake from the towering walls
of the Rift Valley. He knew these winds could capsize the
large wooden canoes used in East Africa and possibly our

small boat. The anguished look on Thaddeus' face tells me we are in serious trouble.

Wind has always been my friend, my ally, encouraging me to be bend when I needed to be flexible, carrying me like a bird while parasailing, catching me and providing a safe landing when bungee jumping, and always providing me with safe moorings.

But now . . .

Thaddeus yells from the bow, "Throw over the gas cans. Rip off the canopy. Now!"

Waves continue smashing over the sides. We are taking on water faster than we can bail.

Are there any positive aspects of drowning in Lake Turkana today? The turquoise water feels warm as it encircles my body. Maybe hypothermia won't set in until nightfall. I shiver when grasping the alternative, Nile crocodiles patiently waiting with mouths open, teeth gnashing, ready to tear into my flesh.

Erratic gusts of wind are filling the canopy and trying to capsize us. Light-headedness takes over. I think about how quickly my life might end here.

Not today. Not this way. I will not die today!

In spite of my five-foot, one-hundred-pound frame, I follow the instructions of the shouting Dutchman. An adrenaline surge propels me as I jump up to reach the canopy. Hanging precariously from the eight-foot-high frame, I loosen the flapping canvas. Another huge gust of wind and water sweeps through the boat. I lose my grip. The churning Jade Sea opens her arms to receive me ...

The Whirlwind of Life

There are, in the heart of the vast Himalayas, some strange marketplaces where one can barter the whirlwind of life for infinite wisdom.

—Jetsun Milarepa, Tibetan Yogi and Poet

Five Years Earlier
1999
Nashville, Tennessee

A blanket of excitement fringed in fear hangs in the atmosphere here in the U.S. I escape to a room filled with the calming scent of lavender. Candles flicker their welcome as I see my reflection in the mirrored doors of an armoire. A purple, velvet-clad, wingback chair calls my name. I'm in the safety of my favorite hair salon. Glancing down, I notice a *Men's Journal* on the marble coffee table by my feet. This cover story catches my eye: THE TWENTY MOST EXCITING WAYS TO CELEBRATE THE MILLENIUM. I grab the magazine and eagerly flip through the wrinkled pages, hoping my name won't be called before I'm able to consume the entire article. Little did I know that as the twentieth century fades into the twenty-first, my future is being imprinted leading me to an exotic place halfway round the world.

I think how my life has been moving forward for the past decade surviving a painful divorce, fulfilling my childhood dream of becoming a park ranger, and following my passion for travel by parasailing in Acapulco, Mexico, and horseback riding through the jungles of Costa Rica. The past six months have been spent on assignment in Washington, D.C., at the US Army Corps of Engineers (USACE) headquarters, where I've been immersing myself in the moving parts of our government. With great anticipation, I'm ready for my next adventure.

All twenty ideas listed in the *Men's Journal* article intrigue me, but three are highlighted in my mind: kayaking across the International Date Line; watching the huge fireworks display in Perth, Australia; and trekking on the Everest Highway in Nepal.

As the days leave me closer to making a decision about where I want to be to celebrate the Millennium, Nepal keeps rising to the top. Mountain Travel-Sobek, North America's oldest adventure-travel outfitter, is planning an exceptional millennium ten-day journey through the Nepalese Himalayas. Participants will start at Lukla and climb for six to eight hours a day up and down scree-strewn trails and through forests of firs and magnolias before reaching 12,680 feet at the Tengboche Monastery. This trip is for me: no electricity, no phones, and no computers. This will be my first big international adventure out of the Americas and into the Eastern cultures of Asia. Leaving behind the doomsday predictions of something called Y2K will be the best part.

Supposedly, everything important is somehow connected by computer programs, and when the clocks turn from the twentieth to the twenty-first century, all will be lost and in chaos. People are stocking up on nonperishables, buying generators, and preparing for the apocalypse. My plan is to be in Nepal trekking, where I can preserve my serenity away from the panic and hysteria that is spreading like wildfire here in Middle Tennessee.

I invite my two sons, whom I love with my whole being, to join me. My oldest son, Douglas, reluctantly agrees to come along. My youngest son, Derek, has made other commitments he needs to honor. I'm disappointed because this would be a wonderful adventure for the three of us. Now I just keep my fingers crossed that my firstborn doesn't back out at the last minute.

My desire to travel to this part of the world began a few months earlier when I watched Tibetan monks creating a sand mandala at the Smithsonian Institute. A mandala is a chart, diagram, or drawing of intricate geometric patterns that symbolize the universe. Achieving the desired pattern takes great concentration and focus. It was a meditation of sorts as monks used wooden, pencil-like tools to transfer colored sand from small silver cups to the design. I sat cross-legged on the floor all that afternoon, mesmerized, and didn't leave until the last grain of sand was in place.

Every so often monks on the sidelines would ring bells to symbolize the progress.

The very next day, the monks ceremoniously released the mandala into the Potomac River to send peace around the world. They presented each person in attendance with a few grains of mandala sand to take home to expand the flow for peace. So what did the monks know that I didn't? It seemed they were so incredibly one with the world, and that's exactly what I hope to replicate by traveling to this remote region of the globe and leaving behind the concerns of Western influence.

My preparations for the trip are full of obstacles. I need a last-minute root canal. My son is disinclined to obtain a passport. A rare parasite enters my body while I'm hiking a remote trail in the Savage Gulf area of middle Tennessee. It takes several doctor's appointments to identify and treat the culprit. Blisters develop on my feet because of my training regimen. Our visas get lost in the mail. An airline cancels our reservations. During a highly recommended stress test and ultrasound, I'm alerted to a heart murmur that's rated as a two on a scale from one to ten; therefore, not a clinical problem but still important information. After all that, I make a trip to the emergency room at Mount Sinai Hospital for a urinary tract infection on the very night before my departure. These hindrances might discourage the uninspired or be perceived as the universe providing signs that I should abandon the plan, as some of my friends suggest. But I see these hindrances, as measures presenting themselves for some unknown reason but, nonetheless, to be dealt with and conquered. A therapist once told me that every time we make a commitment, we will be tested. If that's true, I am abundantly blessed.

I've been in a long-distance relationship with John, one of my old college flames since our class reunion in the fall. My trip plans fascinate him, and he invites me to spend a week at his California home before I depart for Kathmandu. One of my favorite afternoons is spent at Venice Beach interacting with the entertainers on the boardwalk and later playing bongo drums at sunset. At the end of the week, we camp in the caves that wind along the oceanfront and sleep on the warm sand. John, a true Californian, who is into all things natural, encourages me to give up caffeine. He has no coffee in his home. I have him take me to a Starbucks every morning for my starter cup.

Give up coffee?

I think about it, and in the morning, I say, "Why not? I'm always up for a good challenge."

By mid-morning I'm already experiencing withdrawal, a headache, so I seek out a snack machine at the campground visitor center. I'm about to purchase a candy bar, when John suggests I refrain from eating chocolate.

I can't believe what I'm hearing. "Are you kidding me?"

He stoically clarifies his point. "Chocolate has caffeine in it."

I put my money in the slot anyway and I'm ready to punch the button for a Snickers bar, but stop, think about it for a moment, and instead push the coin return. I give in and commit to experiencing the Himalayas, as he puts it, drug-free.

When the day arrives for me to meet up with my first-born at Los Angeles International Airport (LAX), I hold my breath. When he finally comes down the concourse, I hardly recognize him; his long dark brown locks that suit his musician style have been shaved off. He is bald as a monk. But he's here, and I'm delighted. We have time to hug and then head to the gate to catch our flight on Thai Airways. The airline staff treats us like royalty. Even sake is free on our stop in Tokyo, Japan, for refueling.

Arrival in Kathmandu, Nepal is culture shock for a gal and her son who have never spent time in an evolving country in Asia. So many people milling about. So many cars, bicycles, motorbikes, and carts—everyone having somewhere to go. Horns blowing in response to near collisions all around us on narrow streets with no traffic lights. People packing inside and on the tops of wildly painted busses. Street vendors calling out for buyers. Food aromas mingling with exhaust fumes. People bathing nearly naked in the small streams, and a few perfectly uniformed police officers standing by, watching it all. To top it off, we find out that the commercial Indian airliner sitting on the tarmac when we arrived had been hijacked and the fate of the 178 hostages is still unknown. All this scares me and the nine-day trek in the mountains hasn't even begun.

Home for our first two days is the Malla Hotel in the area near Parliament, the Palace, and the Embassies. From here we tour the cities of Kathmandu and Bhaktapur on Christmas Eve and Christmas Day. We're in a part of the world where Hindus and Buddhists prevail; therefore, we see no outward signs of Christian holiday traditions taking place. The only excitement is a policeman chasing someone through the hotel atrium in the middle of the night.

Our trekking begins the next day when we fly to Lukla on Yeti Airlines. We prepare to land on a gravel runway on the side of a mountain. An announcement from the flight crew comes over the intercom: "Do not be concerned since we, your pilot and copilot, have trained on U.S. aircraft carriers." We hold on to our seats as the plane bounces along and comes to an abrupt stop. I'm glad to have my feet back on the ground. My son isn't ready to leave behind the beautiful airline hostess with whom he has made a connection. A group of men covered in dust and wearing handkerchiefs over their noses and mouths sit on the sides of the runway pounding stones into gravel with hammers. I can't help but stare at this bizarre scene.

As the plane begins to depart, the propellers provide a stiff breeze that envelops me. I remind myself to breathe. The motors rev, and the plane bounces awkwardly along the runway preparing to become airborne. Suddenly, it's off, returning to Kathmandu, leaving us in the dust.

Sanjeev, our guide, corrals our group and tells us that we are at 9,000 feet in elevation and must climb down to 7,000 feet to the Dudh Koshi River, also called the Milk River due to its milky appearance, for the night. This river drains the Mount Everest massif, which contains the highest peak in the world. We sleep along its banks and eavesdrop on the melodic rush of water throughout the night while stargazing from the comfort of our tents. What an exhilarating first day.

On day two we begin the real trial: climbing back up to 9,000 feet and beyond almost vertically to over 11,000 feet. This is the toughest stretch. I compare it to being on a Stairmaster for over eight hours, but worse. The rock steps, chiseled into the slope of the mountain, are not only endless, but I believe were made for some kind of giant, maybe the Yeti, a mystical creature that's said to inhabit this area. On the narrow parts of the trail, we trek between a jagged wall of crumbling rock on our left, where one might get caught in a landslide; and a sheer cliff face on the right, where one could tumble into nothingness. Locals haul building materials on their backs and lead overloaded pack animals on these footpaths that they share with us, the trekkers.

Even though we are roughing it because of the extreme climb and cold temperatures, we also have creature comforts. We have our own caravan of yaks that carry tents, cooking supplies, and personal belongings led by a group of Sherpas, who meet our every need. They prepare breakfast so that it's ready when we awake. While we eat and ready ourselves to hike, they load up and get back on the trail ahead to reach our lunch spot. When we arrive for lunch, it's ready. And as we once again eat and rest, the Sherpas trek to our tent camp for the night and prepare dinner. I am so grateful.

When we stop for the required and much-needed altitude acclimation at Namche Bazaar, the Tibetan marketplace, I am jubilant. Namche Bazaar is known as the gateway to the high Himalayas of the Mount Everest region. It's a relatively small town, a bustling tourist zone, and trading hub of the Khumbu region. This stunning village is perched on a sloping hill. The tea houses are colorful, three-story structures, and the shops have interesting signs posted, like THIRD POLE LODGE AND CLUB PARADISE. This is a happy place where paths and people converge. Even Tibetans, loaded with goods to sell or trade, venture over the mountains to this marketplace for business.

We're at 11,290 feet and I have a headache. My thigh muscles are crying out for me to rest, but I muster up the energy to go shopping and purchase a yak bell to remind me of my close encounter with a yak caravan this morning that was carrying supplies across one of the swinging bridges. As I was trying to catch up with my group after a pit stop, I stepped onto one of the wooden slats of a hanging bridge. Keeping my focus on my feet so that I wouldn't fall through the spaces of missing slats, I didn't realize a group of yaks was coming towards me from the other end. When I heard the sound of a clanging bell, I was suddenly reminded of the rules of the road: trekkers must yield to these beasts of burden or be trampled, or worse, pushed off the bridge. I made a quick retreat. The incident was an adrenaline wake-up call to keep me on high alert.

I meander through the cobblestone street at Namche and spy a boy monk in a red robe and sandals. He's eating a chocolate-covered donut. I shout, "Look, he has a donut! Where did he get it?" He looks my way and gives me the cutest icing-smeared grin. Time, temperature, altitude, none of these matter at this moment, but oh to have something sweet with chocolate. Shortly thereafter I come upon a bakery, and there they are - donuts. I buy two, stop for a moment, wistfully think of California John's request, and then happily indulge my cravings. Thank you, Hermann Helmers Bakery, for existing up here baking these delectable treats that supply me with a scrumpous burst of energy.

The Sagarmatha National Park is headquartered here at the end of town, and I'm so hyped to go to the visitor center and interact with their park rangers. They tell me that Sagarmatha is the local name for Mount Everest which means Mother of the Universe.

I'm fascinated their outfits are very much like my park ranger uniform. They are olive drab with identifying patches on the shoulders and gold-plated name tags on the breast pockets. I have fun taking photos with the guys, but am disappointed I don't meet any female rangers.

Trekking normally ends in October as it becomes far too cold for comfort, but this year is special. Three countries have received permits to take groups up the mountain in celebration of the Millennium. We, the U.S. group, sleep in tents. Even though the temperatures are lower at this time of year, the skies are very clear, so we enjoy some sunshine during the day and feel like we can touch the stars at night.

Two doctors are part of our group of sixteen. They are a married couple and have made it perfectly clear that they have paid for this trip and should not be considered 'trip doctors.' In the night I hear a woman scream, "I can't breathe!" It's the lady doctor. Now I don't feel so intimated by the effects I'm experiencing, like a pounding headache and shortness of breath when turning over in my sleeping bag. I learn that the effects of altitude sickness can begin at 8,000 feet. The lower oxygen level available to the body can cause symptoms like headaches and breathing difficulties. The main reason we have stopped here for two days is to allow our bodies time to adjust to the lower oxygen levels. Even so, there is no guarantee one's body will cooperate and produce more red blood cells to transport oxygen to the cells and take away carbon dioxide.

The morning of our departure from Namche, I whisper to my son, "What have I gotten us into?" He finds this to be extremely funny. I watch him happily get back on the trail; he is truly a warrior. Thank goodness he has connected with a couple of young single guys in our group. Every time I see them together, they are laughing.

I head out on the trail but not quite as enthusiastically today. Sherpa Bimba must see my hesitancy and offers to carry my daypack. He has been serving me coffee in the morning. I love how he quickly slips a couple of sweet treats into my hands and holds on just long enough for me to feel his warmth and sense a connection.

Survival at this altitude at this time of year is crucial. The rules are clear. One, drink water. Even though it has been boiled by the Sherpa staff, the water has matter floating in it, and I have to force myself to drink without gagging. Two, eat properly. You can't be too picky here, so I eat what is put in front of me. Three, make it to camp before sunset. This is a must if you don't want to be stranded in the freezing cold without a tent for protection. Four, ward off illness. We have to be careful of food poisoning or bacterial infections, so we wash our hands thoroughly.

I'm grateful I made a trip to Seattle to the Recreational Equipment Inc. (REI) flagship store, where the knowledgeable staff completely clothed and equipped me for this adventure. It's paid off nicely now that I'm here and fully understand the demands of being properly prepared to spend time in the Himalayan environment.

Maslow's hierarchy of needs is tested and proves to be true. Once my basic survival needs are met, I concentrate on interacting with the locals, absorbing the awesome scenery, and balancing my social exchanges with the group to fulfill a desire for acceptance among my peers.

In the late afternoons, flashes of creature comforts begin to flood my mind. Will there be a teahouse tonight with a stove and fire to warm us? What will be served for dinner?

Will there be adequate light so that I'll be able to write in my journal? My biggest challenge is to comprehend that I'm really here. I thank my body for documenting the truth by becoming leaner and stronger each day.

A Canadian couple ends up in our band of sixteen. I shall call them Dick and Jane. Dick is a thirty-something macho man, and Jane is a sweet gregarious girl in her mid-twenties. Each morning when the Sherpa brings water to our tents, Dick bathes outside in the cold with no shirt on. He is loud and boastful as we climb. The rest of us quietly place one foot in front of the other and try to stay connected as an ensemble.

Dick comes down with a respiratory illness and struggles through the rest of the journey. On the days we are on the trail for ten to twenty miles, he surrenders to his tent after dinner. Jane looks lost and bewildered.

To add to these dreaded thoughts of becoming ill in such a remote place in the world, we encounter one of the other groups coming down the mountain one afternoon. Everyone is sick, even the Sherpas. They stumble by in silence, barely acknowledging us. What happened? Sanjeev says food poisoning, since they appear pale and weak. Some are clutching their stomachs. He reminds us of the importance of washing our hands. Trudging upward and onward, I nod well-wishes to the last few stranglers and say, "Namaste," as they pass.

After seeing them struggle, my legs begin to feel like they might give out at any turn. My mouth is so dry, I can't swallow. My lungs struggle to keep air moving. Somehow, I keep on going, thanks to Sanjeev who encourages me, as I push through the discomfort. However, dragging myself into camp last tonight humbles me. In the morning full of new zest, I hit the trail and receive a glimpse of my future in the first rays of sunlight as I climb up this snowy path to the roof of the world. I savor the image. It is intoxicating.

The Tengboche Monastery, the spiritual center of the Sherpas, comes into view at sunset. I can feel the presence of those who came before me, like Sir Edmund Hillary and Tenzing Norgay, who stopped here for their final blessing by the resident Lama before making that first historic ascent of Mount Everest in 1953. I'm so proud of my resiliency for having made it to our ultimate destination.

It's New Year's Eve.

I reflect on all the encouragement I found along the way. First, weathered prayer flags waving in the breeze; second, the miniature Buddhist temples known as stupas, or Chortens in Tibetan, where I would stop for a break, bow in respect, and give thanks for making it thus far; third, the spectacular art on the sheer rock cliffs that temporarily took my mind off the pain in my body; and fourth, the Buddhist mantras hand-painted on the many Mani stones, large and small, that could be found along the trail. All of these inspired me to continue my quest. *Thank you.*

As the sun drops behind the majestic snowcapped mountains, clouds move in, and the temperature drops drastically. There are no teahouses here to warm our hands.

Dinner is served in our dining tent. Our typical meals so far have been porridge for breakfast, tuna sandwiches for lunch, and rice and veggies for dinner. Tonight, we are having yak kabobs, baked potatoes, sweet and sour vegetables, and coleslaw. Cabbage and other vegetables grow well on the lower-level terraced gardens of Nepal.

Later we sing and dance to the beat of drums and drink and hug under the star-studded sky with our travel mates and Sherpa guides. I hang out with my new friend, Bimba. His comfortable demeanor with his infectious smile pulls me in. I discover how wonderful unspoken communion can be. You have to pay more attention to everything else like body language; facial expressions; laughter, crying, or sighing; and the resounding enticement of dancing feet.

At midnight, our cook, Deepak, takes a ceremonial cake out of the smoldering coals of his yak-dung inspired oven. Juggling a large portion of cake in his hands, Bimba presses a small piece with chocolate icing against my lips as if he has seen this done in American weddings.

Enjoying his playfulness, I reciprocate saying, "Happy New Year."

Holding glasses of champagne high, we thank the mountain gods for our good fortune. Welcome to the twenty-first century.

Winds of Change

When you get clear about the things you want, you are giving a definite direction to the way you want gratitude's magical power to change your life, and you are ready to begin the most exciting and thrilling adventure you've ever been on!

—Robyn Byrne

Winter 2000
Himalayas of Nepal

At one o'clock with numb feet, I retire to my tent, but even that does not keep out the winter chill at this elevation. We are near Mount Ama Dablam, which reaches over twenty-two thousand feet. Ice has already formed on the tent walls, and the hand warmers I have slipped inside my sleeping bag don't make any noticeable change in the temperature of my frozen limbs. It is bitter cold, much colder than the Lake Erie winters I experienced as a child.

I start thinking about Dick and Jane and how I approached Jane earlier in the evening. "Come let's have a drink together to celebrate."

She wrapped her scarf tightly around her neck to keep away the night chill and replied, "Sorry, but Dick wants me to spend the evening in the tent with him since he's still not feeling well."

I find this disturbing and think back to what California John said as I was heading out on this adventure of a lifetime: "I have no desire to travel anywhere outside the continental United States." I remember watching Westerns with my father as a young child and thinking, *I want to be the one who climbs on the horse and rides off into the sunset.* I fall asleep with this thought percolating in my head.

In the morning, New Year's Day, I awake to the low growling of the long horns that call the Buddhist monks to prayer. They also summon me. I shyly enter the monastery. A giant golden Buddha statue sits cross-legged behind flickering shadows cast by numerous candles in iron candelabras. A monk wearing a large animal-skin robe ushers me to a seat on the floor and offers biscuits and tea with yak butter, which I slowly ingest. I laugh at the child monks running in late to take their places on the wooden benches. Some wear sandals and they try to wrap their feet in their long robes to keep out the cold.

The prayer service, *puja*, includes chanting, playing of ancient musical instruments, and blessings. The musical charm and intonations warm my heart. At this moment I feel an alliance with the cosmos; it's pure enchantment. And in a strange way, my future becomes clearer: (1) moving out of the Southeast, (2) meeting my significant other, (3) living in my dream log cabin, and (4) traveling to remote ancient sites.

Arriving back at my tent grounds me. Our gear has been loaded, and the group is ready to depart. As I grab my daypack, I pull Sanjeev aside. "I saw a small sign on the wall of the monastery this morning. It tells of old cymbals that the monks are willing to sell to support the renovation of their living spaces. My son, an accomplished drummer, will be enthralled and won't want to miss this opportunity."

Sanjeev leads the two of us inside the private area of the monastery. It is dark and gloomy. Tea is served as the monks play a variety of cymbals. Douglas hears the sound he wants to replicate and settles upon a pair of cymbals that are three-grandfathers old. We make a sizeable donation, for us, of $100 each. The Rinpoche, wearing crimson and saffron robes, thanks us by placing blessed scarves around our neck and shoulders. We bow in awe and respect.

Our troop has been waiting patiently and is anxious to begin the trek downhill, back through the villages of Phakding, Namche Bazaar, Thame, and Khumjung. Within four days of what feels like free-fall, we glide down the trail and finds ourselves back in Lukla having a party while we wait for the weather to clear so the plane that will take us back to Kathmandu can land.

Throughout the trip, I have avoided the local brew, the rice chang of Nepal, but now I'm ready to shout *Cheers*. In Lukla, I hear of a way to give back to my new Sherpa friends through the American Himalayan Foundation, a nonprofit that supports schools, hospitals, and clinics in the Everest region and beyond. *Thank you.*

Saying goodbye is difficult. Hugs all around happen quickly, and we have to scramble onto our plane while the engine is still running. We go bumping along the freshly spread gravel, and I marvel at how quickly we become airborne. My last glimpse of the Everest region and my new Sherpa friends is through the airplane window. I wave and wonder if I will ever see them again. Bimba smiles and I remember how I would grin every morning when he came to my tent as I greeted him, "Namaste. Coffee, please."

I will be forever grateful for that wonderful liquid elixir discovered in Ethiopia and to the Germans for making those delectable chocolate-covered donuts all the way up in Namche. Coffee and chocolate never tasted so good, and I will never take them for granted again.

Back in Kathmandu at the Malla Hotel, I enjoy a series of showers to remove all the layers of grime from walking ten days on the dirt trails, basically the same clothes. Then I indulge in a two-hour full-body massage that's not only well-deserved but what I badly need to relax the strained muscles, tendons, and ligaments throughout my body.

We have one more day for sightseeing and souvenir shopping, but first we plan our lunch at the Rum Doodle, where on our arrival in Kathmandu we had the best noodle soup. Later we will have dinner at the Yak & Yeti, where I'll once again get to enjoy my favorite Nepalese dish: *momos*, a pan-fried dumpling that comes with a variety of fillings and is served with a spicy dipping sauce. I can't get my mind off food today.

We catch a ride to the Monkey Temple, a sacred place where deities and monkeys are protected and fed. I'm climbing stairs once again, and muscle memory kicks in with dread, but this time the end is in sight. I have forgotten that there are crackers in my backpack. A derelict monkey jumps from a tree onto my back and leaves me screaming in fear. He is able to unzip my pack and jumps off with the stolen crackers in hand. I've surely made my contribution to the cause.

Our next stop is in Patan at the Tibetan Refugee Camp, where Tibetan carpets are handwoven. I purchase two small carpets tied with 100 knots per inch from 100 percent Tibetan wool. One is decorated with the crisscross monastery symbol, the other with the symbol of wealth, health, and prosperity. The sales lady says, "Fixed price for a good cause." *I agree.*

In the evening I walk the back streets of Thamel with my son and our new friends and am surprised when we are offered street drugs from the locals. We don't accept, but others on the trip are disappointed that no one offered them any.

In the morning we are on a plane to Thailand. There we spend the night at the luxurious Amari Hotel in Bangkok. Tired but not wanting to miss the action, I book an evening tour of the city. I enjoy the lights, the ornate shrines, and the vibrant street life.

I must come back here.

We land safely at LAX the next day and find out there was no Y2K after all and yet in some remarkable way, Y2K has been a gift that led me on a path of outward and inward exploration. Now I experience reverse cultural shock: a rude airline hostess, impolite passengers, and cell phones ringing everywhere upon landing. I'm highly irritated by the noise level in the airport.

John was hoping I would join him for another week at his home. I saw him as a sort of hero in the past because he was a revered athlete and the adventurer who went on a hitchhiking backpacking trip to Mexico for a year before beginning his career. I admired the way he had orchestrated his life. This trip has tested me physically, mentally, and emotionally and I'm proud of the way I'm choreographing my life as an independent woman. After getting my bags, I head to the transfer desk to book an immediate flight back home. The last flight for the day leaves in thirty minutes. I find a pay phone and call John. No answer. I make a quick stop at Starbucks. An announcement comes over the PA: Final call for Flight 409.

I pull a page from my journal and quickly scribble a note:

Dear John,

Timing is not on our side. Thanks for everything. Heading home. Wishing you a long, happy life.

Goodbye.

I leave it at the information desk. As I'm running down the concourse with a Starbucks Mocha Frappuccino Grande in one hand and my boarding pass in the other, I hear the announcement over the PA system: "Paging John Ross. Please come to the information desk to retrieve a message."

Driven by a Northwind

Your heart knows the way.
Run in that direction.

—Rumi

Summer 2001
Smoky Mountains National Park, Tennessee

Waking up in the middle of the night, I quietly slip out the door of the cabin I share with four other hikers. A meteor streaks across the sky and plunges down through the body of the Big Dipper. What an incredible occurrence and what extraordinary timing.

After arrival back in the states, I was restless. Thoughts of joining the Peace Corps resurfaced from my college days. Wouldn't it be great to be able to return to Nepal as a Peace Corps volunteer? I applied.

Meanwhile, I also wanted to explore other parts of our vast country, so I applied for a competitive park ranger position with the U.S. Army Corps of Engineers in the Northwest. After a series of group interviews, I was chosen by the Seattle District team. Then, of course, I heard from the

Peace Corps. They offered me a volunteer opportunity to teach in Nepal. *Decisions!*

I told myself that the Peace Corps would always be there but this competitive park ranger position may not come back around. So, I made my choice and I'm spending my last week in the Southeast with friends enjoying one of my favorite places, Mount Le Conte in the Smoky Mountains National Park. Amazed and thrilled, I believe that seeing this shooting star in the night sky is just further confirmation I'm making the right decision to move across the country. The vision I experienced in the Himalayas is already manifesting in my life.

*

One week after seeing the shooting star, I say my goodbyes to Tennessee. I'm driving my Jeep Wrangler Sahara on my way to Idaho, and my son Douglas is riding shotgun. I share how I'm channeling my character from the play I wrote way back in the seventh grade called 'Go West or Bust.' My English teacher had me read it to the entire student body, and even though I was a shy teenager, I was proud to divulge my adventuresome spirit.

Douglas and I make a point to see as many national parks along the way as possible. I especially enjoy driving into Yellowstone National Park without a reservation for the night. The staff apologizes that they only have one room left and it's in the old section of the Old Faithful

Lodge. I laugh because this is exactly what I'd hoped for. On another day, we have the best breakfast at the Gourmet Truck Stop restaurant in the Gallatin National Forest: blackened rainbow trout served over an English muffin with poached eggs and hollandaise sauce. This may be the best eggs Benedict I have ever had. Douglas especially enjoys our stop at Devil's Tower in Wyoming because one of his favorite movies was filmed there, *Close Encounters of the Third Kind.*

On our fourth day, we find ourselves traveling on the winding Going-to-the-Sun Road in Glacier National Park in Montana. Our trip has taken us through several states and past iconic national treasures like Mount Rushmore, the Badlands, and the Grand Tetons.

When we cross the Long Bridge into the small Idaho town of Sandpoint on beautiful Lake Pend Oreille, something shifts in my body like the Libra scales balancing. We have reached my destination: a new town, a new job, a new life. This isn't my first time to cross this bridge. A year earlier I had done the same while on an assignment for park ranger training and had the same feelings arise. I'm supposed to be here.

Douglas helps me unload my carry-type belongings into my hotel room. When I drive him to Spokane for his flight the next day, we see a billboard advertising Tremors, one of the top-rated wooden roller coasters in the country. I say, "Shall we?" and he says, "Yes." So we make a quick stop at the Silverwood Theme Park and pay the entrance fee just to ride Tremors. It is crazy fun. I don't realize now how much I'm going to miss him and the rest of my family and friends. But my professional life in the Southeast had become stagnant, and I craved a new beginning.

Spending a month in a hotel on the shores of Lake Pend Oreille while waiting for my household goods to arrive is like being on a long vacation. During the day, I'm enjoying meeting the ranger staff and tackling my new assignments. Both my supervisors have a huge amount of confidence in my decisions as director of the visitor center, and they put me in charge of a major renovation. I work on a plan to finish off the lower level with a conference room and office space for my staff. I'm grateful for my background in interior design and joyously immerse myself in this exciting project. I also begin training the summer rangers to assist during the major camping season in the area. At night I try all the ethnic restaurants within walking distance and lay in bed watching the sailboats crisscrossing the water as the sunset dissolves into the waves.

When the moving van arrives from Tennessee, I comprehend the enormity of the change I have initiated and find myself crying and sobbing all weekend. My heart aches for all I have left behind—my family and friends, business associates, favorite parks, restaurants—all things familiar. I immediately send invitations to everyone I know to come and visit.

Lucky for me, I meet Jessica, a kindred spirit, a lover of nature and adventure. She moved here from California and manages rentals in the area. She arranges for me to occupy one of her duplexes in town. I quickly learn that the town and its residents highly value hiking and biking. I've been told you can leave the keys in your car at night and nothing will happen, but if you don't have your bicycle locked up, it will more than likely be gone when you wake in the morning.

I hadn't ridden a bicycle in years, and my first purchase in this unfamiliar land is a mountain bike. I act like a teenager, riding with no hands. Now that I'm back in snow country with sledding and cross-country skiing, I rejoice in the activities of my childhood spent in the snow belt of the Great Lakes. The Northwest is agreeing with my connection to the natural world, and I begin to see the benefits physically and emotionally.

The Canadian Rockies become my go-to place on my days off. Jessica becomes my tour guide for the next year, and we indulge in road trips most weekends exploring the mountains and lakes in the area. When I win a whitewater rafting trip for two on the Salmon River, it doesn't take much for Jessica to agree to join me for the week. Sleeping on the riverbanks at night under the stars and running the rapids every day heightens my awareness and catapults me back to the adrenalin rush of living on the edge that I experienced when trekking in the Himalayas. All of this meshes comfortably with my enthusiast personality.

When Jessica asks me to join her to train and participate in a mini-triathlon called the Lake to Forest, which comprises a quarter-mile swim in the ice-cold lake, an eleven-mile mountain bike course through wet-weather streams, and a three-mile uphill run, I hesitate. Eventually, I say yes. But I must admit the six months of training were more exhilarating and challenging than the actual day of competition. That day, with my eagerness to get on the road to Canada with a visiting relative, I end up leaving before the awards are handed out. I came in first in my age group. I didn't realize I was the only one in my age group participating but I still wear the medal proudly.

I love my life here.

A Whisper in the Wind

Let us be thankful for those who make us happy for they make our souls blossom.

—Ivorian proverb

Fall 2002
Sandpoint, Idaho

A aron enters my life as a gentle breeze, one that wraps itself around me like an embrace from an old friend.

I have told family and friends that even though I would love to be in a relationship I won't go out and seek one. The man will have to come knocking at my door. Being divorced for some time, I'm dedicating all my energy into living out my childhood dream of being a park ranger. Then on a pleasant summer morning in this small town there is a knock at my door. I peer out the kitchen window and see my good friend Jessica, who owns the duplex, standing there with a nice-looking gentleman.

The doorbell rings, and I open the door.

"Hi. I would like you to meet your new neighbor, Aaron."

A new neighbor. Please let this be a positive person with positive energy.

A large family with pets had occupied the smaller side of this duplex, but they had been evicted a few weeks earlier. I immediately hired the local shaman woman, Ann, to bless the house and sweep away all the negative energy and make room for only positive people with positive energy. Ann lit candles and prayed. I threw salt into the corners of each room, as prescribed.

"Hi, won't you please come in for some coffee. It's from Starbucks."

Aaron with a warm smile politely says, "May I have a rain check?"

Feeling disappointed, I respond with a flippant, "Sure, any time."

The time comes when a group of Maasai warriors from Kenya visits our town. Aaron knocks on my door again. "Would you like to join me this evening for the Maasai performance at the Civic Theatre?"

I haven't been to the restored theatre yet and am thrilled by his invite. Plus, now I will have an opportunity to get to know him. We enter the playhouse, and I feel like I'm in the ornately decorated theatre in Cicely, Alaska, in *Northern Exposure*, my favorite TV show. Here we are, Aaron (Joel) and I (Maggie), sitting mesmerized as the warrior's chant and display remarkable jumping skills.

Aaron is engaging all evening and introduces me to some of his good friends who are there volunteering at the ticket and concession booths. On the way back home, as we stroll through the darkened streets dimly illuminated by torch lamps, our fingers gently brush against one another, and I feel an incredible charge of electricity.

Aaron stops by for coffee most days. It becomes a ritual we enjoy sharing. We hike in the mountains, sit out on our shared patio in the evenings, and talk into the early morning hours. When the weather turns cold, we walk around town in the evenings to keep warm.

The holidays are coming, and I look forward to spending them with him, but first, I make a trip back to my hometown for Thanksgiving to be with family and friends. Then with Christmas approaching, Aaron tells me he'll be going to California to spend a week with his stepson.

I had high expectations for spending the holidays with him, but I say, "I understand. I hope you have a great time."

He replies, "I will be back to spend New Year's Eve with you."

He sounds so sincere and reassuring. A smile comes over me. "Thank you."

I busy myself over the long holiday by working and spending time with Jessica and her family. I even arrange a trip to one of my favorite towns, Coeur D' Alene, and book a hot stone massage at the resort. I decide to take a public van so that I won't have to worry about parking. When I enter the van, the driver starts chatting with me, and I find out that he knows Aaron quite well since Aaron uses his van often when going out of town.

Now he asks, "Are you Aaron's California girlfriend?"

I'm stunned and not sure how to respond.

I finally say with disdain in my voice, "No, I am not her."

The driver, embarrassed, remains silent for the rest of the trip.

When Aaron returns on New Year's Eve, I'm ready to confront him. He left ten days ago, and I'm still trying to process the new information that was gifted to me. He fesses up. "I went to California to break up with my long-distance girlfriend."

"So you didn't go to see your stepson."

"No."

"You lied to me."

"Yes, but I am here with you now, and you are the only one I care about." He reaches for me and kisses me passionately. I forgive him in the heat of the moment, and we make love for the first time.

At breakfast the next morning, I study his features. His graying hair and deeply lined face contrast with his youthful physique, creating an elaborate sculpture. I'm attracted to this intriguing contradiction: the body of a surfer dude from California combined with the weathered look of an explorer in the wilds. I want to spend all my time with Aaron, but I need my focus and energy on last-minute details for a trip to Africa.

Having been a park ranger in the Northwest for nearly two years now, I'm happy to have made the acquaintance of others in my career field through the National Association of Interpretation (NAI). NAI is passionate about supporting those who interface with the public to understand the value of our shared natural and cultural heritage. Individual members include those who work at parks, museums, nature centers, zoos, botanical gardens, aquariums, historical and cultural sites, commercial tour companies, and theme parks.

NAI is planning their first international eco-tour: a safari to Kenya through Origins Safaris, operated by Steve Turner. The closest I have ever come to going on safari is when I was on assignment in Washington, D.C. I participated in the Snore & Roar program at the National Zoo, which entailed a wine-and-cheese icebreaker, a midnight stroll through the park, and a continental breakfast the next morning after sleeping on Lion Hill.

Now the real thing: The departure date for NAI's safari is in less than one month. This is an opportunity that I cannot and will not miss. Even though I'm still getting to know Aaron, I toy with the idea of inviting him to join me.

Clouds Sweeping Low, Drifting High

*Enchanted places have the power to change us, to
germinate and nurture that tiny seed of happiness…
that each of us have kept so carefully concealed.*

—Alexandra Campbell

February 2003
Kenya

A aron is able to join me on my adventure after getting permission from his mother, who controls the family trust fund. This 'Mother may I' scenario is another one of those occurrences in my life where yellow caution lights flash in front of me but I choose to ignore them.

Traveling as a couple presents challenges that I could not have foreseen. Our adventure starts out with a bizarre turn of events, and I begin to think I've made a huge mistake by inviting Aaron to join me.

We fly to London to meet up with the rest of the group. The trip leaders, Bob and Mary, are there to greet us. Mary immediately takes a liking to Aaron, and this makes me happy; he will fit in and feel comfortable. But when we have our fourteen passengers ready to board the plane to Nairobi, one of the female rangers, Cindy, panics and white-knuckles the railing. "I can't go. I'm too frightened!" she shouts.

Before Mary or Bob can respond, Aaron runs over to her and says that he will escort her onto the plane, which he does. We find our reserved seats in economy class. Then Aaron says to me, "Here. Take her boarding pass and give her yours so that she can sit by me and I can walk her through the fear."

"What?"

"Yes, just give her your boarding pass for now. This will only take fifteen minutes or so."

"Really?"

"Please."

In shock, I take her boarding pass and move farther back to my new seat. I'm in the middle section of the Air Bus seated by Mary and Bob.

They laugh and say, "Hey, we are happy that your boyfriend just took over for us."

After one hour, I'm tired of sitting here. Actually, I'm quite furious about the whole situation. Part of me says, *You should be impressed by Aaron's compassion for another human being and just suck it up.* But the other part says, *hey, you invited him to be your companion, and now you've been thrown under the bus.*

Over an hour and a half goes by. That's it. I've had enough. I say my adieus to Mary and Bob and make my way up to the front section where Aaron is sitting in his reserved seat and Cindy, Ms. Frightened, is sitting in mine.

"I would like to have my seat back now."

"Oh, okay," she says. She moves into the aisle and then adds, "Is he your husband or just your boyfriend?"

Who is this person?

My body is shaking from being on flights and in airports for the past sixteen hours, shaking from barely any sleep for the past twenty-four hours, and shaking from the emotional drain of this bizarre development.

Later in the trip, I find out that the only reason she came on this safari was to find a new boyfriend. Even when we have to be in a safari vehicle with her during game drives, she sits there with her eyes closed. She continues to be a source of stress for me because of the way she keeps vying for Aaron's attention. She's a source of comic relief for others because of her peculiar behaviors like walking around on the tarmac at airports.

After landing in Kenya and on the way to our hotel, I spy a giraffe majestically striding through the grasslands in the open spaces beyond Airport Highway. It's riveting to be in the presence of African wildlife so soon and so close to the city. I'm overflowing with anticipation. Our safari guide gives me a thumbs up.

We stay at The Norfolk Hotel the first night of our safari. Built in 1904, the hotel continues to be one of the most beloved landmarks in the city and the launch point for bucket-list-worthy safari tours. We are thrilled to be staying here, but staff warns us not to walk out on the street in front of the hotel. So, this is exactly what Aaron and I do on our first morning after breakfast. We walk right out the front door of the hotel and find The Cultural Center (Opera House or Performing Arts Center) is across the street, and farther down towards town is the University of Nairobi. Aaron, being anxious to converse with Kenyans, leads us to encounter people as they make their way to their jobs or to the university. Everyone is extremely friendly and surprised to see visitors out walking. The university students who speak English are happy to congratulate us for taking the 'supposed risk,' as they put it.

Aaron and I definitely have one thing in common; we do not let fear of strange places rule our lives. The Norfolk has wonderful gardens within the compound and there are plenty of paths for leisurely strolls that we also enjoy.

The National Museum of Kenya is situated behind the Norfolk and the Boulevard Hotels, and we can easily walk there. But no. We are told we must ride in safari vans. Many of these restrictions were put in place after the terrorist bombing of the U.S. Embassy in 1998. I begin to understand this point of view. They are just making sure tourists are safe.

The museum aims to interpret Kenya's rich heritage and offers a one-stop for education and leisure purposes. The botanical gardens also provide a serene environment. What I enjoy most at the museum is the collection of Joy Adamson's watercolor portraits of members of the forty-two tribes of Kenya. Her array of colors and attention to detail are exceptional. She is also known for the story *Born Free* about Elsa, the lion and the movie based on her story that I've watched multiple times.

I'd been looking forward to visiting the beautiful Ngong Dairy in a suburb of Nairobi called Langata, "the place where the cattle drink," according to the Maasai. Ngong Dairy is the house used in the film *Out of Africa*, the story of the life of Karen Blixen, the Danish novelist. One of Blixen's famous lines is: "I will remember Africa; will Africa remember me?" I would have to say, they certainly have, since the coffee served on her once well-known coffee plantation is first-rate. I also enjoy a banana split with my cappuccino while sitting on the patio and absorbing the serenity that surrounds this place.

We ride in safari vehicles out to The Samburu National Reserve, where our first game drive occurs. The highlight for me is seeing a leopard stretched long and heavy, high in a tree. Her spotted legs drape over a branch, and her dangling tail appears to be swinging in rhythm with her beating heart. She is at an ideal place on this sunny day with her young kitten snuggled under her chin and barely visible from our vantage point.

The Buffalo Springs National Reserve is next on our agenda. It is a protected area in the Isiolo County in northern Kenya. The desert rose is found in the scrub with bright pink blooms. The toothbrush tree provides food for elephants, and the nomadic Samburu people use its twigs to clean their teeth. I could spend days watching the elephant matriarchs protecting their young as they wade through the swamps of this area.

A narrow country road takes us to Lake Naivasha. At 6,181 feet, it is the highest elevation of the Kenyan Rift valley. The name Naivasha is derived from the local Maasai name *Nai'posha*, meaning "rough water," because of the sudden storms that can arise. Ironically, a sudden storm arises between Aaron and me while at a Valentine's dinner dance at the hotel. Right in front of me, Cindy, Ms. Frightened, asks him to dance, and he accepts. Jealousy takes me hostage. While trying to free myself, I whisper a few choice words when he returns to our table. "Did you have to say yes?"

He, frustrated, jumps up and heads back to our room without giving me an answer. I proceed to stay out late with my new friends. When I slip back into our room, he is asleep. I'm grateful because I'm not interested in more drama.

In the morning all is forgotten. It's a new day and we are on our way to the Lewa Wildlife Conservancy (LWC). This conservancy addresses the increase in poaching and black marketeering that has caused wildlife numbers to suffer. LWC decided to take action and provide a reserve to protect animals like the rhinos. Aaron and I are back in a natural setting where we both feel most comfortable. As we stroll from our tent to the observation blind to view black and white rhinos, I gaze at Aaron beside me. He has this rugged environmental entrepreneur look, like he is capable of saving the world. This is the man I want to love and whom I want to love me. As he gazes back, I wonder how he envisions me?

Origins Safaris has booked us at a riding stable. Our horseback ride is among zebras, antelope, and giraffes. Even though I'm quite afraid of horses, I climb aboard and give my life over to a raucous stallion. Aaron, an expert horseman, stays close by, which is reassuring. We are briefed: You have to move carefully. You have to be ready for any event, like a horse bucking after a snake strike or when a lion bursts out of the grass to protect her young.

For us today, it is an elephant in the bushes. I am panic-stricken.

Our guide whispers, "Prepare to make a run for it."

Oh, no! If I have to gallop my horse, I will bounce right off and be trampled.

In what seems like an eternity, we gently guide our horses in a different direction, keeping our eyes fixed on the moving branches. Then we hear the trumpeting. The ground trembles. It is so close. Adrenaline surges into my body. I don't dare look back to see if we are being followed, but at some point, I feel we are safe.

Suddenly, I begin to giggle, and laughter grows amongst our small group of riders as the high alert that one feels in dangerous circumstances gives way to relief that the immediate danger has passed.

Aaron grabs my hand and holds it tightly, murmuring, "Oh my God."

Each day is a new adventure, and today we pay a visit to Samatian Island where Rothschild's giraffes are protected. Eight giraffes, four females and four males, received a rare lift to their new home, leaving the savannah behind. These endangered giraffes—only a few hundred remain in the wild—were ferried by barge to a reserve on this island in Kenya's Lake Baringo. We are able to walk around the island with young giraffes, so it looks like the plan to save the species from extinction is working.

*

I have butterflies in my stomach this morning. We take a predawn ride in the Land Rover out to Governor's Camp, where pulsating flames illuminate two hot air balloons. Here in the Serengeti Plains of Africa, I can't think of a better place to take my first ride. I'm told that the sun on the equator always rises at six. The morning moon is setting in one direction, and the sun is rising in the opposite as we get underway. Aaron remains on the ground and takes some great photographs of the balloons rising. Then he goes on a game drive with the others who have opted to stay safely grounded. Ms. Frightened latches on to him. This time jealously does not take me prisoner, and for the moment, I'm independent and no longer tethered to Aaron. I'm my own person and one with the wind. I'm confident. I trust in myself to make good decisions. I'm flexible. I have the ability to bend and see all sides of an issue. I give myself permission to change my mind and head in another direction if that is what is best for me. And I'm free, free to soar and reach great heights.

We skim the tops of the yellow fever trees as the first rays of the sun touch their bark, turning them a gold-green. Floating high above the ground, I'm wild with happiness. The hot air blasts spook the antelope, and they scatter like misbehaving shards in a toy kaleidoscope. The giraffes just look at us out of the corners of their eyes and keep on munching the tree leaves on the uppermost branches. I don't want this experience to end. But the balloon starts to drop, and we land, awkwardly, in a reclining position on the ground. I'm not sure if I should be alarmed since we're being pulled along through the savannah by the wayward balloon. Abruptly, we come to a stop. Trying to climb out of the tipped basket is a spectacle.

I hear corks popping and see a table covered in fine linens set amongst the plains. Brunch awaits us. We clink champagne glasses and quickly consume the quiche and strawberry shortcake. What a wonderful climax to an amazing adventure.

On our last night in the Maasai Mara Reserve, I awake to a crunching outside our tent. The stillness of this moonlight night amplifies the sound, and Aaron is already awake, watching through the tent's netting.

He whispers, "There is a large, dark silhouette standing between us and the river."

"I think it's a hippo," I whisper in his ear.

I can't believe how close she is to the tent and how big she is—probably between 3,000 and 4,000 pounds. Afraid to make the slightest movement, Aaron and I are both still like mannequins. She is munching on the scant amount of grass surrounding our tent. I wasn't aware that hippos spend their nights foraging on land. What a surprise! At first light, she saunters down the mud path on the riverbank and enters her daytime habitat in a gigantic splash. We snuggle together exhausted but savoring the closeness we have had with the natural world here in Kenya.

On the last safari day, Aaron and I sit near the edge of the riverbank having breakfast, when joyful tears spill down my cheeks. "At this moment it feels like we are the only two people left on earth, and here we are together in this incredible place." I reach for Aaron's hand across the small inlaid table.

He gently squeezes my fingers and points to a family of hippos that have surfaced and are splashing in the water only a few yards away. Then our eyes shift to the other side of the river where baboon families are chattering in competition for their daily breakfast delicacies. Soon we are laughing, as two grey louries flit over our heads screeching a mantra: *go-away, go-away*, hence their common nickname, go-away birds. It reminds me of an old nursery rhyme, and I sing, "Ladybug, ladybug, fly away home."

"Your house is on fire and your children are gone," Aaron joins in.

How is it that we both remember such a funny children's rhyme at the same time?

As we take our last sips of coffee, the rumbling sounds of elephants so close to camp awe us. Aaron and I are hooked on Africa. I'm curious if hooks have also been set in our relationship, hooks that may cause pain and suffering later.

But now I've seen the Big Five on my first safari: lion, leopard, elephant, rhino, and Cape buffalo. There is an African saying: "Once you drink of African waters, you will return to drink again." I am hopeful.

As we depart the Mara Reserve, I make eye contact with a handsome warrior. He gives me a devilish half-grin and I reciprocate. There is something striking about his demeanor. He gives off a feminine air because he is so beautifully adorned with beaded jewelry, but his tall, muscular frame flaunts his manhood. A Kenya wildlife officer, who is standing guard, sees this interaction and says, "He's from the Maasai tribe."

Then I remember the Maasai warriors who danced in our small Idaho town a few months ago. At that time, I knew nothing of the beat set in motion by their feet as they chanted, nor did I understand the pulsating of their bodies in rhythm, and certainly not of the traditions surrounding their jumping. I notice the officer smiling at me, and he playfully adds, "They are fine warriors and said to be great lovers."

"Really!"

Caught in a Crosswind

*I truly believe that regret is the only wound from
which the soul does not recover . . .*

—Sarah Ban Breathnach

Spring 2003
Sandpoint, Idaho

S oon after arriving back from the Kenyan safari, Aaron and I take some time to enjoy an incredible spring afternoon at the lake. Sitting close together on a wooden bench overlooking the water, I confide in Aaron, "I regret not joining the Peace Corps right after receiving my bachelor's degree." He looks at me like I'm crazy, but I'm serious. "I wonder if it's not too late for me to fulfill this twice-missed opportunity and join the Peace Corps in Kenya?"

A look of concern comes across Aaron's face. He turns away from me and gazes out to the water and the Selkirk Mountains in the background. Slowly he turns back in my direction and speaks in earnest. "Please don't join the Peace Corps."

"It's only for two years, and then I will come back here."

He takes my hand in his and continues, "I can provide a similar experience for us in Kenya."

"How can you do that?" I search his face for some expression.

He stands, puts his hands in his pockets, and paces in front of the bench. "I've been thinking about this, and I have enough money to finance a one-year stay for both of us."

A motorboat comes whizzing by and we are momentarily distracted. The wake splashes water up at our feet. "But what would we do?"

"Maybe you could teach school." Aaron is still pacing.

I stand up and step closer to the rocky shoreline. The water is pristine. I can see schools of small fish.

"Schoolteacher, huh?" I haven't thought about teaching since I left that field years ago. It was never my first career choice, but I was steered in that direction by guidance counselors. I face him. "But what will *you* do?"

"I will photograph. Photojournalism has always been a dream of mine."

We both skip stones as the water calms.

"Remember the baobab trees?" I ask. "You could do a whole coffee-table book on the diversity of those ancient spiritual trees."

"Good idea. I would love to do that."

"So, are you really ready and willing to go to Africa for a year?"

"Yes."

I put my arms around his neck and rest them on his rock-solid shoulders.

His sharp jaw line moves with his speech. "I love you. Isn't that reason enough?"

I think of a saying I heard on the streets of Kathmandu in 2000: *"Opportunity comes; but does not linger."* Here is my opportunity, no more regrets, a year in Africa and with my new man!

All we need to find is a partnership in Kenya. This turns out to be the easy part.

We contact Steve Turner of Origin Safaris and he has the perfect fit. We will operate out of the Taita Discovery Center (TDC), an educational facility in the middle of the bush near Tsavo National Parks and participate in his wildlife and community programs. Because I'm a park ranger, he alerts the local communities and sends me a list of projects that I might be willing to accept: writing and editing a newsletter for the Kasigau Conservation Trust; organizing a bike derby with the Taita chief to gain support for promoting conservation in a human/wildlife conflict zone; participating with the planning and design of a visitor center at the Tsavo East National Park gate; and being a consultant for the Lumo Community Wildlife Sanctuary, which is in the beginning stages of planning a grand opening for tourism. I also hope to get a chance to teach a program certified by NAI that I present to seasonal park rangers in the United States each spring. Either way, I'm hyped about the role I will be playing in Kenya. Aaron will be free to photograph at his leisure and assist me whenever possible.

During one of our phone conversations, Steve laughs and says, "When Kenyans hear that you work with the U.S. Army Corps of Engineers, they have huge projects in mind for you. Like replacing the fifty-year-old water pipeline that goes from Voi to Mombasa. Or building a bridge to connect Tsavo East and Tsavo West National Parks." Steve introduces us to Dick Mills, the owner of World Discovery Safaris in Birmingham, Alabama and Dick assists us in finalizing all the necessary paperwork.

Meanwhile, I begin the arduous task of applying for a one-year leave of absence from my park ranger position. It is Memorial Day weekend. Aaron and I want to move in together so we take up residence in a small log cabin overlooking a shallow, spring-fed lake on his mother's property. Now, really? Here I am living in a log cabin with my significant other; both reminiscent of the vision I had in the Himalayas.

Aaron's mother lives in the big house high up on the hill, which is in view of the cabin. When we started dating, Aaron asked his mother if she approved of me. She responded, "She's a keeper." We occasionally have dinner with her, and I wonder if she still feels the same now that I'm moving in with her son and planning a year-long stay on another continent, with her providing the financial means.

I sell many of my possessions and make several trips to the local Goodwill to downsize. Then I begin to focus on this monumental African undertaking. Aaron and I believe that the universe is miraculously supporting our goals and dreams of adventure while providing us an opportunity to embrace global cultural diversity.

*

M eeting with the park manager, my supervisor at our project, and sharing my idea of procuring a leave of absence from my park ranger duties for a year leaves me frustrated.

I'm denied over and over. Each time I come up with a creative solution, the answer is still the same. Mid-summer arrives, and I'm still the only one convinced that the Kenya experience will make me a better park ranger. I feel I'm involved in a serious game of poker. Each time I meet with the other players, I'm forced to show another card. I toy with the thought of playing my trump card. It's an ultimatum: if you won't sign my request for a leave of absence, I will leave my position as park ranger.

Am I really ready to make this kind of decision?

Not long ago, I was newly divorced and jobless. At that time, I mulled my situation over and received an answer from my inner child. She reminded me of a declaration I made at age nine on my family's first trip to Allegany State Park on the border of Pennsylvania and New York. After participating in a critter race sponsored by the state park ranger staff, which included a female ranger, I announced, "One day, I am going to be a park ranger."

My younger self's dream somehow got buried, but the erosion of life uncovered it. This 'knowing' changed my life forever. Within two weeks of reconnecting with that vision, I was a park ranger sporting a Smoky the Bear hat and living the life I was meant to live.

And now I'm struggling to take advantage of another incredible opportunity and not lose my dream job in the process. My proven track record of dedication to my duties over the last few years makes me confident I'm valued in my work. So, I keep pushing and don't *fold my hand* at the poker table.

A new Chief of Operations has just been hired, a woman from New England. Her reputation precedes her; she is known to be tough. My superiors have asked her to take over their seat at the table regarding my request. I suspect they're confident she'll also decline. After making her decision, she sends a project-wide email saying, "Have a great adventure on behalf of all of us."

My relentless determination has paid off, and I'm thrilled to know I'll still have my job when I return.

Healing Breezes

My vision can be so limited. I often think that the only outcomes are those that I can imagine

—Courage to Change

Summer 2003
Abadiania, Brazil

Aaron suddenly adds a whole new dimension to our plans of spending an entire year in Kenya. He has waited until now to share that he has a severe seizure condition. I find out the seizures were the reason he rented his side of the duplex when we met one another in the town of Sandpoint. He'd lost his driver's license because of the condition and needed to be in town where he could walk everywhere instead of out at his family's compound in the country. As a teenager in California, he suffered a surfing accident. He remembers riding a large wave and then seeing his board first flip up in the air before crashing on his head. He doesn't remember anything else until he woke up lying on the beach with his friends standing over him.

I'm shocked and sorry for what he has endured and not sure how to interpret this new information. I'm frightened. Will it be safe for us to be in Africa on our own? What role will I need to play in this? Then Aaron surprises me again. This time with his determination to be healed before we leave for Kenya. My apprehension eases.

Word is making its way through our small town about a healer who lives in Abadiania, Brazil. A few local acquaintances are preparing for a trip to see John of God, Joao de Deus, the healer who performs miracles. One of Aaron's close new age friends is encouraging him to join the group of emotionally charged individuals, and he asks me to go along.

I don't have any major physical ailments, but I hear myself say, "Yes, I'll go, but only to provide support for you." Plus, who could say no to a trip to Brazil!

*

Today we receive a briefing about the trip since we will be leaving in just a few days. For the past fifty years, John of God has been a dedicated and powerful spirit-healing medium and psychic surgeon. I learn that psychic surgery doesn't require any anesthesia, and supposedly it doesn't even hurt.

As a teenager, John went to a river to bathe. He says a spirit of a radiant woman, who later turned into a ball of light, told him to go to a nearby spiritual center. Later, according to John, this same spirit was identified as St. Rita of Cassia, Brazil's patron saint of miracles. John says he remembers following her instructions, finding the center, walking up the stairs, and knocking on the door. He doesn't remember anything else until he regained consciousness hours later with a circle of people standing over him. According to him, he supposedly had healed the people through the spirit of King Solomon. Afterwards, he says, he stayed on at the center, compelled to dedicate his life to healing others and to never accept payment for his work.

*

We arrive in Sao Paulo, Brazil, on a beautiful, warm, sunny spring afternoon. We take a two-hour taxi ride through the countryside to the Casa de Dom Inacia. Our accommodations at the bed and breakfast are a minimalist's dream. At dinner John of God's assistant meets with our group to explain what will happen tomorrow. She suddenly looks at me with a wonderful smile and says, "The spirits are already working on you." I'm stunned.

As we walk back to our rooms, Aaron asks, "Why you, when I'm the one who came to be healed?"

I'm not sure how to address his concerns, so I just take his hand in mine and say, "I don't understand what's happening either."

At dawn we are instructed to dress in white. This will allow the spirits to see into and through each person clearly. I wear white just so I won't stand out in this sea of foam floating down the dusty road between the village and the church.

When I arrive at the healing sanctuary, I wander around the garden atrium. The well-manicured and creative landscaping is impressive. I walk along the flagstone paths winding through a variety of local tropical plants and flowers. Some hummingbirds flit nearby and butterflies alight on the foliage. I remain on the fringes and watch as the believers form a long line in the courtyard.

Eventually I wander through the throngs to a latticed entrance and spot a note posted off to the side of the main cathedral door. It is a letter from the 14th Dalai Lama to John of God. The Dalai Lama very eloquently gives his blessing in support of John of God's work. This gets my attention. I'm a huge admirer of this Dalai Lama. The Libra scales are starting to tip. I look around and assess the situation. *Will one more person be a problem?*

After all, the spirits are already working on me, aren't they?

I surprise Aaron when I jump in line with him and the rest of the flock anxiously waiting to meet the "healer." Soon the cathedral doors fling open, and I strain to see the man. I'm amazed at how quickly we are moving. Before I even reach him, he is looking at me through lightly tinted glasses. He is of average structure, has dark brown hair, and is wearing a brown suit. When I'm finally in front of him, he's no longer looking at me but at someone behind me. He scans the line, similar to the way a Sherpa scans the trekking trail, letting the mind record the terrain ahead so the eyes will not have to look down when they arrive at the spot.

Since John only speaks Portuguese, an interpreter encourages us to ask for a cure. Since I do have a minor heart murmur and a slight scoliosis of the spine, I decide to make my request simple: "Provide for me whatever it is that I need."

We are herded along out the side door. An usher leads me across the atrium to a set of crystal beds located in a small structure along the edge of the garden area. I'm separated from Aaron and feel anxious. Here I lay on my back with a machine moving crystals back and forth about a foot above me. They hover over my chest, reminding me of alien spacecraft from a science fiction movie. I laugh and try to get serious. The entire process takes most of the morning. Lunch back at the villa is fresh fruit and vegetables. I rejoin Aaron, who's been in the meditation rooms all morning. We eat in silence.

Afterwards, I'm ushered back to the crystal beds, where I mutely agree to let them continue with the interrogation of my physique, a process that lasts well into the afternoon. Aaron continues to spend his first day in the meditation rooms. Our leader tells him he must let go of his ego if he wants to benefit from this experience. He's visibly upset and remains subdued all evening.

The second day of our adventure takes us past John of God once again, and this time I'm taken to the 'current rooms.' I'm told that this part of the treatment is essential because the spirits that work through John of God also work in these places. The healing entities are spirits of deceased doctors, surgeons, masters, and saints who have been exceptional people during their life on earth. No one knows which ones will appear on any given day.

Here we sit in the stifling heat on hard wooden benches in silence for hours. We are told to sit with our feet on the floor, shoes off, hands facing up in our laps, and our eyes closed, regardless of what is going on around us. My attention span is so short; I find myself opening my eyes and peeking around the room. We are warned that a guard on duty will tap us on the shoulder or even remove us from the room if we lose our concentration. Luckily, I avoid both.

In the afternoon a window is opened in the current room, and I can feel the hint of a draft of air. I hear a young child weeping and someone mumbling a prayer. I also overhear music floating into the room on the scant breeze. The very large person sitting next to me smells of old sweat; it is smothering and it takes all the resolve I can muster to stay in the current room this afternoon.

After three excruciating hours, we are given permission to leave. Words don't seem adequate to describe how happy I feel to be out of that place. The walk back to the villa is glorious. I dance in my head. A white chocolate and macadamia nut ice cream cone after dinner is a well-deserved treat. Aaron, once again, is in the meditation rooms for the day. He remains withdrawn in the evening, and I can't seem to break through the barrier he has put up between us.

On the third day, I'm asked a big question: "Do you want a visible or an invisible operation?"

I could forgo both options and just go back to the room, but a part of me is curious.

"Invisible," I say. I'm a bit nervous, but I follow several white-clad people to the operation room. Again, we are required to keep our eyes closed.

"Put your hands over the area of the body that needs healing or over your heart," a coach says. "Some people will feel nothing and think that nothing has been done. However, an x-ray will show internal stitches or a tumor gone."

I place my hands over my heart. I have to admit I feel some fluttering in my chest during the process and wonder if my heart murmur is being mended. We are handed instructions as we leave 'the OR' and cautioned against talking about our experiences. I take a taxi back to the villa and begin my required twenty-four-hour rest period— no sun, no lifting, no exercise, and no long walks for eight days.

I stay on at the villa and follow my instructions. I have ice cream every day, even though I'm lactose intolerant. Surprisingly, I don't have any issues. When I mention this to a dietician on site, she tells me it's because all the food is blessed before it's served.

On the seventh night after the operation, I read over my critical instructions. I wear white to bed and pour a glass of blessed water to keep on the nightstand. Before going to sleep, I invite the spirits to come and remove the stitches. I sleep for eight hours. In the morning, I drink the glass of water.

I have been resting and following the rules for eight days. I've enjoyed short walks around the grounds and today I receive special permission to hike to the most beautiful waterfall. I suspect this is where John of God may have encountered the spirit woman.

On the ninth day, I go back to see John of God in the "revision line." I'm anxious to see if he will release me to go home. He gives a nod as I pass, and I'm released. *Hooray!*

The only requirement left is to spend the next forty days—considered to be the healing time—minus alcohol, pork, hot chili peppers, and sex. Apparently, if I don't comply, the benefit of the surgery may be compromised.

Just as I start packing to leave, I hear a commotion out in the hallway of our villa. Aaron tells me that one of the women in our group is hemorrhaging. I have no idea what surgical procedure she had or how it was performed, but I'm afraid for her. Along with the shouts for help are whispers for silence. Help arrives just as I depart alone in a taxi to Sao Paulo. I'm worried for Aaron and don't want to leave him behind. We've hardly seen one another since arriving. We knew that would be the case, but now with everything going on, the separation is painful.

Once back in Sao Paulo, I have a few hours until my flight departs, so I ask my driver to take me on a tour of the city. Our trip down Paulista Avenue takes us past the Sao Paulo Art Museum with its bright red columns supporting the glass structure that sits seventy feet in the air. It's an amazing model of modern architecture. In contrast, the Casa das Rosas, a French-style mansion, sits among ornate gardens in the middle of one of the largest cities in South America. With the hustle and bustle of excitement all around me, I ask my driver to make a quick stop for a traditional cheese-filled donut from a street vendor. The nourishment relieves much of my anxiety. Donuts have aided me before.

*

I spend more than a week alone at Aaron's log cabin on the family compound. I have only spoken to his mother briefly to let her know that Aaron was required to stay on for further treatments. When he arrives back in Idaho, he calls me to pick him up at the airport. Now I will finally have answers to some of my urgent questions. He assures me that everyone in our group is healthy, doing well, and returning home, but he is reserved and not willing to discuss his experience. I'm sadly disappointed. In fact, he has very little to say except, "I will not be giving up the meds for my epilepsy." Aaron and I continue with our trip plans for Africa and no longer speak of our Brazil experience.

Note: At the time, there was no way I could have known what was about to come to light in 2016–2019. Around the time of the #MeToo movement, John of God surrendered to authorities on charges of rape and sexual assault after more than 100 women filed complaints.

Part II

A WHIRLWIND YEAR IN AFRICA

Tell me, what is it you plan to do
with your one wild and precious life?

—Mary Oliver

The Colors of Africa

*I don't want to be reasonable—there is plenty of
time for that in the grave. What I want is adventure,
innovation, foolishness and discovery.*

—Mirabel Osler

Fall 2003
Kenya, Africa

O n our last day in the states, I'm obsessed with taking
a long, hot shower. I rearrange my bags over and over
again, eliminating items and then repacking them. I have
purposely not consulted with anyone that has been on an
extended stay in Africa so that I'll be able to have the experience without preconceived notions.

Aaron and I leave our family and friends somewhat in the
dark regarding where we will be living, what we will be doing, and how to get in touch with us, mainly because we don't
have all the answers either. Aaron's mother is visually upset
at our departure. She gives me a side embrace and avoids eye
contact. We leave her waving goodbye in the driveway.

I haven't asked Aaron about the financial arrangements
he made with his mother, the bank, their accountant, and

his financial advisor. I'm trusting that the details have been well thought out and planned accordingly.

I'm grateful to be heading out with my partner Aaron to live a life of adventure. We make a last-minute stop at McDonald's so we can share a Big Mac. After checking in for our flight, I savor a Mocha Frappuccino Grande in the airport Starbucks.

I try to picture the Taita Discovery Center in Kenya. It lies between two national parks, Tsavo East and Tsavo West, on land that's in a private and community-based trust. Steve Turner says that TDC is a perfect destination for those who wish to help establish the largest private wildlife sanctuary in East Africa. The aim is to provide scientists, educators, local communities, students, and conservationists access to each other and a vast wilderness in which to work, study, and explore.

TDC is approximately sixty miles from the nearest post office and internet service, and we will only have the opportunity to visit there every two to three weeks. I plan to try to keep in touch with family and friends by phone if and when we have cell service. We will buy a phone when we get there and hope for the best.

*

A fter watching old movies for eight hours out of Amsterdam, I raise the window blind from my seat on

Kenya Airways. As we begin our descent, I can clearly see glimpses of life on the plains through the pure white clouds. There is smoke billowing from the small huts laid out on a circular canvas of monochromatic colors. I can't help but wonder who lives there. What are they cooking for dinner? Will I meet them someday and will we share a meal?

As we approach the city of Nairobi, the tin roofs of Kibera sparkle from the sun's reflected light, and I have to strain to see. Here is where over a million people wake up daily to pursue the dream of good fortune that might come their way if they get a chance to live and work in this capital city.

When we land at Jomo Kenyatta International Airport, I'm nervous. As I step off the plane onto Kenyan soil, my body relaxes. I'm back in Africa. I can't wait to see the baobab trees silhouetted against the clear skies, enjoy the sweet aroma of mandazzis in the markets, sip on coffee and mango juice at the Java House, and listen to the melodic sound of Swahili being spoken everywhere.

I wonder if my love affair with Africa and my love affair with Aaron are inescapably intertwined. I have no inkling how this will play out. Aaron and I have been singularly focused and enjoying all our time spent together preparing for our adventure. I'm still amazed we have found one another in this lifetime. I have high expectations that these feelings will continue as we prepare to spend twenty-four/seven together in a developing country. But for now, I'm just anxious to catch a taxi and collapse at the Boulevard Hotel for the night. Tomorrow I will surrender to whatever else lies ahead.

*

Afiter a light breakfast, our taxi driver is back to take us to the bus-staging area in downtown Nairobi. The chaos is frightening. Of course, it is only chaotic to us, I'm sure. When our bus driver tosses our newly acquired, hard-cover luggage containing our computer equipment and cameras into a compartment under the bus, we cringe. He tells us to get off at Maungu.

"Did you hear that, Aaron?"

"Not exactly. I guess we will have to just keep watching for signs along the road."

The bus speeds away without us having any idea of how far we must go before exiting. We find ourselves surrounded by Africans, and no one is speaking English. Now we regret not learning Swahili, the common language for all forty-two tribes in Kenya, as a part of our trip preparation.

All I know for now is that we are on our way to TDC, the educational complex in the middle of the savannah of the Kasigau Conservancy. Steve Turner's cousin, Leigh, runs the educational center. I have read that one can see many African animals on game drives at the three watering holes. The prime conservation effort focuses on elephants, with 300 to 400 in the area. I hope to participate, along with performing my other duties, in a significant wildlife project that will reflect the goals and objectives of the trust.

Overwhelmed by the high-noon equatorial heat and the fact that none of the windows on the non-air-conditioned bus will open, we are thrilled to finally get a break after four agonizing hours. I search for a restroom. My thigh muscles have a flashback: *Oh, no! A squat toilet like the ones in Nepal.* I became accustomed to them there, so I can do the same here and deal with burning and cramping thigh muscles.

Aaron is becoming acquainted with a few women of Indian descent who are dressed in beautiful multi-colored saris and wrapped in matching shawls. They share a snack similar to bridge mix with him.

"Help yourself," they say as I take my seat.

I'm afraid to indulge in this strange-looking food, but my low blood sugar makes me reconsider. "Thank you," I say as I grab a handful.

Two hours later, the bus comes to a sudden stop. A sign says MAUNGU. The warped door of the bus squeaks open, and I climb down the steep steps on wobbly legs. The young bus driver unceremoniously tosses our suitcases on the ground, and we are left standing in a cloud of dust along the Nairobi–Mombasa Highway.

What a sight! Lines of open shops with tin roofs adorn the sides of the street for fifty yards in both directions. Trucks or lorries, as they are called here, creep along bumper to bumper on the shoulder of the road like a python slinking through the dirt. They send clouds of choking dust and exhaust into the crowd. I sense that the colorfully dressed locals are stopping their daily activities in favor of watching us.

What are they thinking?

I feel lost, unsure of what we should do next. Then I hear a voice in the distance, someone calling my name from an open Land Rover. A staff member from TDC waves like an old friend. I excitedly climb on board and relax for the thirty-five-mile road trip to TDC. My body bounces to and fro as we proceed down the muddy, potholed road.

We come to a security checkpoint and rangers armed with rifles stop us and check to ensure our names are on their approved list. I survey the situation as smoke rises from a firepit near their tent-style housing. We are entering Rukinga Ranch, a wildlife conservation area owned and operated by a Canadian gentleman. As we continue on, I spot a herd of Cape buffalo on our left. They stop grazing and watch us intently as we maneuver a curve in the road on two wheels. Mount Kasigau looms in the distance, rising 1,600 meters above the Taru Desert in the Eastern Arc Mountains. The peak is best known for its rock outcropping called Cobra Rock.

Upon arriving at TDC, we drive along a tree-lined dirt landing strip. A torn windsock struggles to fly in a shallow breeze. An earthen dam springs up in front of a dry pond, and acacia trees circle the entrance to the Center. The air here in the heart of the plain is pure and vivacious. Birds chirp and call out to alert others of our intrusion into their sacred space.

The staff of eight greets us. They can't hide their amazement at the size and weight of our luggage. Leigh, the manager, welcomes us with a handshake and leads us to a circle of thatched-roof huts called *bandas*, or rest houses. Our banda is made for two. Fresh linens cover the camp-style beds, a small table holds a kerosene lantern, peg hooks call out for clothing, and tab-style café curtains cover a screened window and a fairly modern bath—including a European-style toilet. I'm delighted.

Chef George, a happy-go-lucky person, prepares a late-afternoon snack and delivers it to our room. It is the most delicious cheese and tomato sandwich I think I have ever had. *Thank you, George.*

We only venture out of the comfort of our banda when we hear the dinner bell ringing. We walk along a stone path lit with lanterns. The open shelter sitting in the middle of an oasis gives one the sense of being in a rainforest rather than the harsh savannah. Meals taken here become one of the highlights of our time at TDC. We enjoy the ambient lighting, the smell and taste of international fare, the soft breezes and light rains, the roar of Tsavo lions, the grunts of elephants searching for water, and the stimulating conversation that awaits all who enter this sanctuary.

There is talk of sending us to a banda-type structure, one that has no electricity or running water, in the village of Rukanga at the foot of Mount Kasigau for the entire year.

Leigh says, "This way you will be providing some income to boost the local village economy."

But then we would be living 'in the bush.' I'm confused about how I'll be able to complete my assigned tasks, and furthermore, I like TDC and would be perfectly happy to stay here. After dinner, as we sip Irish coffee, Leigh suggests we climb Mount Kasigau tomorrow. Feeling refreshed after hot showers and a great meal, Aaron and *I agree.*

At 6:00 a.m. there is a knock at our door. "Time to get up," sweet Leigh gently calls out.

Exhausted not only from traveling but also from the long hours spent planning this trip and working a full-time job for the past six months, all I want to do is rest in a hammock for the next week. But no, we are back in the Land Rover driving through five small villages to the Mount Kasigau trailhead.

The trail starts out like most, with a sign and a dirt path. Before long, though, I find myself having to crawl over rocks, hang onto tree limbs and roots, dig into the cool clammy earth with my fingernails, and claw my way up the crude trail. The vistas of the valley and villages below are spectacular as observed through the dense forest. One can see the plains for miles through this important elephant dispersal area between Tsavo East and Tsavo West National Parks.

Leigh and our guide, Simon, whisper, "Stop. Listen. It's the endangered white-eyed Taita bird."

They are thrilled because the bird is endemic only to this area in the Taita Hills. We even catch a glimpse of its white eye ring as it flies over our heads. We make the summit and are surprised to find we are inside a cloud forest. It is lightly raining, and visibility is limited. I believe Aaron and I have impressed our new friends with our stamina and endurance on the trail. Coming down, I go slip-sliding through the mud-sodden trail and once again need to grab onto small trees and bare roots to save myself from disaster.

Spotting giraffe, antelope, and a pair of secretary birds on the way back is an added feature on only our second day. My body is tired, but I feel energized.

On day three, we have a meeting with a representative of the East African Wildlife Society (EAWLS). I believe his name is Malachite. Using my park ranger knowledge and my design background, I'll be joining a team that is planning a visitor center at the entrance gate to Tsavo East National Park with the Kenya Wildlife Service. Aaron and I will be serving as guest editors of a conservation newsletter called the *Kasigau Conservationist* and as business consultants for a newly formed, locally owned reserve sanctuary at Lumo. We'll also be part of the planning committee for a bike derby with the Taita chief. We nod our heads in agreement, blissfully unaware of the difficulties that will arise following through on all these commitments.

After a game drive with some loud visitors that arrived today, Aaron and I have our first argument. "I'm almost out of cash," he says.

I stare in disbelief. "So how have you planned to get us more money from the states?"

"I will have to call or email my accountant to wire some money once we get back to the nearest town."

I realize that we have been spending money for incidentals connected to travel. But finding out that he has limited cash on hand already and doesn't have a concrete plan in place on how he will get more funds from the states leaves me frustrated.

Our first trip to the nearest town of Voi is with Leigh on Saturday. Aaron is able to wire his accountant, and now we will have to wait for a Western Union cash transfer to take place.

I catch a glimpse of Maasai men congregating in the town center. When we stop at the Tsavo Park Hotel, a good watering hole for travelers, a Maasai named Kiyenni greets us with the most genuine smile. What a nice welcome.

I'm amazed at some of the modern conveniences here, like scanners in the small grocery shops. There is even a computer store called Ashtech where we can check email, but they have no electricity today. We are in the minority here as residents, but everyone is friendly and interested in us. Lunch is at the Distar Restaurant, with hamburgers and French fries on the menu. I follow Leigh and try a local dish, ugali with greens. Aaron and I watch a football game, actually soccer, in an outdoor venue. Later, giggling African children surround us while Leigh buys supplies for camp.

We have a fun and relaxing Sunday but on Monday morning, Leigh announces, "It's moving day."

The thought is unnerving because I'm not ready to leave the comforts of TDC. We load up the Land Rover and are driven back over the deep potholes. Five villages with a population of 16,000 Africans, mostly from the Taita tribe, surround Mount Kasigau. The villages all lack electricity and running water. We're informed that one Peace Corps worker, Heather from Arizona, works at a clinic in the area.

We drive into the village of Rukanga, considered to be the capital of this area, unload our luggage, and begin a trek up a narrow solitary mountain path. We pass a springhouse where local women are filling water containers. They all utter, "Jambo." Children wave.

The climb is steep and difficult as we each carry a heavy suitcase with our overloaded backpacks weighing us down. Leigh suddenly stops at a dark, dingy, small clay hut that appears to be in the throngs of crumbling to the ground. I worry that it's our new home and I'm ready to say, "Please don't unload my things, because I cannot live here." But instead Leigh readjusts the luggage he is carrying and turns right onto another dirt path and we climb higher. Rounding the next bend, something amazing happens: the air is lighter and my mood changes. We are in a land of paradise, a tropical forest at the base of a rock-faced mountain. I can't believe the beauty. This is a writer's dream come true. I can picture Hemingway here.

Our new home is a round, thatched-roofed hut, approximately twenty feet in diameter. A wall through the center separates the kitchen and sitting area from the bedroom and storage room. The common concrete/mud walls are open halfway up with screening continuing around the entire structure.

The garden area is beautifully landscaped with palms and cactus. Verbet monkeys are playing hide and seek, running in and out of the plants. A combination of wood and stone makes up an outdoor sitting area. I take a quick glance into the outhouse with shower and toilet and shut the door immediately. I will deal with this later.

The TDC employees drop our bags and say goodbye. They leave us a small shortwave radio that we can use to alert a person in the village for an emergency. We are left alone in the bush. We are both excited and edgy, settling in for our first night. From our windows we can see the plains to the west and east, and straight up the mountain to the north.

We lie in bed, and Aaron shines a flashlight up onto our high-pitched grass ceiling. We have an entire eco-system over our heads: spiders, geckos, and rodents all living the good life inside our new home. We pull the covers up over our heads and hope that sleep comes. A tree hyrax screams as the equatorial darkness envelops us.

Day One: Living in the Bush

Laugh when you can, apologize when you should, and let go of what you can't change. Kiss slowly, play hard, forgive quickly, take chances, give everything and have no regrets. Life's too short to be anything but happy.

—Unknown

Fall 2003
Mount Kasigau, Kenya

I awake to cool air as the first rays of sun brighten the horizon. A humming of activity begins. Birds sing in chorus and roosters crow their wakeup call. A matatu, a minivan, blows its horn down in the village, calling those who want to catch a ride to Voi town. It seems in Africa everyone wakes up at the same time. I look over at Aaron, who is pretending to still be asleep. I tickle him.

He laughs. "Well, we made it through the night without any critters falling on us."

"Amazing," I add.

The noisy horn of the matatu fades as it continues on to the other four villages, all connected by one winding dirt road circling the mountain.

I speak the names of the other four villages: "Jora, Bungule, Kiteghe, and Makwasinye." Then I hear footsteps approaching. "Aaron, do you hear that?" Then someone knocks at our door.

I jump out of bed and peek through the screen. A Taita woman stands on our doorstep with a large bright yellow plastic container on her head. She sees me.

"Hodie, I'm Jasmine."

I slowly open the door and say, "Hi."

I'm not sure what to do next. She points to a barrel sitting in the corner on the dirty cement floor of our banda.

Once again, she says, "Hodie."

I invite her in. She empties the container of water into the barrel and then asks, "Do you need more?"

Actually, I'm not sure, so I say, "No, but thank you, Jasmine."

She adds, "I will see you tomorrow morning."

Aaron comes out of hiding, and we giggle some more. He figures out how to light the propane burner and boil the water, even though Leigh has told us it comes from a natural spring high up on the mountain.

We have been dropped off into another place and time. Now what? We unpack the food TDC brought with us yesterday. Thank goodness we have a bag of ground coffee and a French press. This is the first order of our first day in the bush. Second is to begin cleaning up our living space. We make a list of things we will need to make this a doable proposition like a tub for washing clothes and dishes, couch pillows to soften the wood-slat sofa, and a bedspread for color and comfort. A top priority is a mosquito net to surround our bed here in the Taita Hills of Kenya.

After making toast in a skillet for our breakfast, we walk down the hill to explore the village. When we pass the elementary school, children come running to greet us: "Jambo. Where are you from?" We shake their little hands, as their teacher, smiling at us, encourages them to return to the outdoor classroom.

The dirt and gravel road through this tiny village is flat, with five open-air shops on each side. We meet Kent and Julia who own the first shop at the bottom of our hill. They are a sweet couple with two young boys. It's nice to know that Kent has the other shortwave radio so we can be in contact if necessary. We purchase a Coca-Cola from their newly installed cooler operated by lighting paraffin and ammonia. Somehow that provides a minimum amount of cooling but it's a modern convenience in an area with no electricity that makes the couple proud. We enjoy a leisurely conversation. The one thing that impresses me most is the amount of love and respect they have for one another.

Kent does not hold back. "Julia is the love of my life," he says. "I wouldn't want to live without her."

She smiles and pulls him close.

Farther down the road is a butcher shop with fresh, or not so fresh, meat hanging out in the open with flies buzzing around. We wave and move on to a mercantile-type store where we find some of the items on our list, including a beautiful bedspread. *Hooray!* I'm so happy to try and make our banda as comfortable and homey as possible.

Grace runs the shop, and her husband, Matay, makes weekly trips to Nairobi and Mombasa to purchase the items for the store. She is adorable. Her blind mother sits comfortably in the shade of a scant tree, listening and smiling.

We find a small restaurant nearby, sit down at one of the picnic tables, and order tea and sandwiches. Chickens roam around at our feet, pecking at crumbs from earlier in the day. As I take my last bite, a young man approaches and introduces himself. "Hello, I'm Gabriel, and I would like to be your tour guide."

"Great," I say with a huge smile.

"When you are ready, I can introduce you to the Guy Rock area and take you to the source of our water that is high up on the mountain."

"Oh, to the spring. Yes, we would love to go exploring with you, wouldn't we, Aaron?"

Aaron, not overly enthusiastic, says, "Yes. How about tomorrow?"

"Okay, I will meet you here tomorrow. Say about 10:00 a.m.?" Gabriel moves away from our table, smiles, and gives a modified salute.

At high noon, the coolness we felt in the early morning air has been replaced with an oppressive dry heat. As we head for higher ground, a matatu comes flying by and covers us in fine red soil.

Once back at our new home, I challenge Aaron to a competition. I fill a small jug with water, and we try to balance it on our heads and walk through the garden. It's impossible for us to carry it more than three or four feet, but having the water drench us is a delight, and once again we are laughing.

Word is spreading about our arrival, and Heather, the Peace Corps worker, comes to welcome us to the village. We hit it off immediately. She is from Arizona and is having a mid-life crisis, so to speak. "I had just gotten out of an abusive relationship," she admits, "and I needed to get out of the country."

We both find it interesting that the Peace Corps would station her in the hottest part of Kenya when she had requested a cool climate. She is living on a meager salary as part of the Peace Corps' plan to be fully immersed in the culture.

"My original plan was to join the Peace Corps," I tell her. "Now I'm feeling much better being here on my own terms, or almost on my own terms."

Around dinnertime, we hear another knock on our screen door.

"Hodie, I'm here to cook your dinner," says a woman who introduces herself as Tempest.

"Oh, okay."

I invite her in, and she uses the one burner on the small propane stove in our kitchen area and prepares our first dinner in the bush: *ugali* (corn meal) with sautéed vegetables, the staple of the Taita tribe. The flavor is good, with a spice I have seen her using called Rocco. I invite her to join us, and she does. She lives in the village with her husband and three children. She says she loves to cook.

"Thank you, Tempest, for a lovely dinner."

"See you tomorrow," she says as she is leaving.

Before we know it, the sun is setting. From the twig bench in our front yard, we watch it drop behind the horizon.

"Aaron, I hear someone coming up the trail."

"So, do I. What's in store for us now?"

Williamson and Hateb introduce themselves as security guards for the village of Rukanga. They are from the Taita tribe and tell us they will be spending their nights sleeping in the shed adjacent to our banda.

Hateb says, "Williamson and I will be splitting shifts so that you will have twenty-four hours of protection."

I guess one might say they're the village police. I don't know what we are being protected from, maybe wild animals. The guys sleep on the ground in a shelter made of twigs. They begin cooking their dinner in the hut over a small fire.

As night descends upon us, we light the kerosene lantern and place it on the table made of three large slabs of stone. The light isn't adequate for our Western eyes to see clearly. Even though we are tired from the excitement of the day, seven o'clock is too early to go to bed. I remember the deck of cards I purchased in Heathrow Airport buried deep in my backpack. I excitedly shuffle them, Aaron cuts the deck, and I deal. This is the beginning of a game of rummy that will continue for several months under candlelight here in the bush.

Surviving in the Bush

*Life, for all its agonies . . . is exciting
and beautiful, amusing, and artful and
endearing . . . and whatever comes after it—
we shall not have this life again.*

—Anne Morrow Lindbergh

September 2003
Mount Kasigau, Kenya

J asmine begins to confide in me. "I'm raising three of my children here alone in the village," she says. "My husband lives in Mombasa with our three youngest children. He left me a year ago and said he would take the youngest, two girls and a boy, with him. I have the oldest, both boys, to help me live here in the bush."

Tempest is sweet and fun and loves to cook, but with way too much lard for us. Eventually, I say, "Tempest, we love you and appreciate your cooking for us. But in America, we are used to cooking for ourselves. Actually, I enjoy cooking, so I will take over those duties. Would you like to help me with some special projects?"

"Yes, I'm happy to do whatever you need."

And so it is. She helps me with cleaning and sorting projects, and at times, I sit with her at our rock slab table enjoying Kenyan coffee, munching on stale biscuits and helping her write letters to some of her friends in England. She tells me all about her children, but when I ask about her husband, all she can do is make awful faces. She knows that this always makes me laugh, and so this is our secret.

When she has finished her letters, I always ask, "Did you write about your husband?"

She smiles and shakes her head convincingly, "Hapana, no."

One day she comes running to me. "Mama, do you have abortion pills?"

She is quite upset about the possibility of being pregnant.

"Tempest, sorry, I don't have abortion pills."

When I inquire about her status a few weeks later, she says, "Oh, I was not pregnant after all." I'm happy to hear this and give her a warm embrace.

Williamson and Hateb tell us they are used to making sure people from other countries participating in TDC programs don't have any unfortunate incidences that would affect tourism and the programs. We are grateful, and since the nights have been chilly, we give them our TDC blankets for warmth and comfort.

Early on, Williamson presented me with a hand-carved dipping tool and stirring spatula for our cooking. Both

Hateb and Williamson work hard at making our garden area useful and beautiful. They even construct a gate from tree branches that have fallen during high winds during the drought.

Everyone here is anxious to meet us, and we accept an invitation to visit the local elementary school where the students will perform a traditional dance. The children are excited as they run to shake our hands. I enjoy their presence and videotape their performance. They parade in a line with an air of pride in their steps. A young girl leads the line dance and sings. We plan to debut the video for the children and staff once we purchase a video player in Nairobi.

Aaron has been trained in karate and begins to show Williamson and Hateb some of the moves. He is so relaxed in our new environment and treats everyone like family. I become more compassionate following his lead.

Heather lives like a traditional Taita and rides her black mamba bike to the five Taita villages that surround Mount Kasigau. She even dresses as a Taita woman with a kanga wrapped around her to respect the culture we inhabit. She lives in the village in a small space with no ventilation. After visiting our banda and seeing our new bedspread for keeping the chill off at night, she finds a small house to rent that sits out in the open.

Heather works with people who have HIV and teaches health in the local school. I'm shocked when she discloses a practice that is taking place here. "Can you believe that some of the women have told me that men are pouring bleach into their female partners' vaginas so that they can have dry sex?"

"What?"

"It's true. So many women are experiencing pain and serious infections."

This practice, along with female circumcision, which I hear also takes place, are atrocities beyond my wildest imagination. Who comes up with these ideas?

Everything here operates on African time. A meeting scheduled for 10:00 a.m. might start after lunch or not at all. Communication, many times, is by runner, and traveling anywhere takes all day. There are no vehicles in the village, so we rely on a TDC vehicle when it's not serving as an ambulance, taxicab, cattle or goat trailer, fruit and vegetable truck, school bus, or police van. Mostly we travel to meetings by matatu, a minivan that holds up to twenty people. After it's crammed full, the driver, more often than not, high on the local weed, miraa, speeds over severely washboard roads.

I can remember seeing these vans during our NAI safari and remarking to Aaron, "I can't imagine having to travel like that!" And now I'm here traveling like that!

Trips to TDC are meant for recharging our computer and camera batteries, but our bodies need recharging too. Pampering our cravings for balanced meals of protein, vegetables, fruits, and of course, sweets restores us. So does catching up on sleep and indulging in hot showers. We thought the staff would be picking us up weekly and transporting us to TDC, but that is not the case. We are on our own most of the time, and just adapting to our new environment keeps us busy. Our projects are always on the forefront of our minds, but many times they end up on the back burner, simmering as they patiently await an opportunity for us to take some action.

One evening our dinner is at the local high school headmaster's house. We are served a rooster that crowed a greeting to us when we arrived. Even though I was only able to take a few bites, I had an enjoyable time with the family. Our plan from now when invited to dinner is to say, "Yes, we will come, but we are vegetarians." This will also ease our hosts concerns to know that we will not be expecting a meal with meat.

When I'm in the village and pass the outdoor butcher shop with meat, either roadkill or something poached in Tsavo National Park during the night, I try to look the other way. But invariably the butcher will call out, "Mama, some meat?"

"We do not eat meat." I can almost taste this lie in my mouth as I speak but I don't know how else to address this sensitive issue.

Living without modern conveniences like electricity, telephones, and running water is within my capabilities. Sweeping gecko droppings every morning off the table and floors of the banda is not something I love to do, but I can accept it as a part of living in the bush. Even using the outdoor toilet, really just a deep hole in the ground, and the outdoor shower, a barrel of lukewarm water dumped over my head, is doable. But dealing with the lizards that live in-side the shower and outhouse is something that I can hardly bear. Once, a large black spotted lizard jumps, or falls, onto my back as I'm exiting the swinging door.

"Get off me!" I scream.

Williamson, Hateb, and Aaron come running. Wrapped in only a towel, I'm quite embarrassed. I vow to carry a long pole with me to chase the lizards off when I need to use the loo or shower. Aaron accompanies me when he feels like be-ing sweet, especially at dark when I'm the most disturbed with the situation.

We learn to cook over the propane burner and create skillet casseroles like Spanish rice and canned tuna with noodles. We have even figured out a way to make pizza. The brown flatbread from the Muslim grocery store makes a great crust. I even made a pineapple upside-down cake for dessert one day.

Hateb and Williamson have made us bows and ar-rows and tools for cooking and cleaning the Kenyan way. When Williamson hands me a long-handled broom he has made, I hug it. Now I won't have to bend over while sweep-ing, something customary for the locals. Sweeping is like an Olympic sport here. Everyone is out in the morning haze vigorously pushing the dirt from one place to another. Once I accomplish that, I wash clothes with Omo, a strong deter-gent meant to remove the red soils of Tsavo.

In the afternoons, I see women hoeing in the vegeta-ble gardens called shambas. If the men have no immediate business concerns, they can be found congregating togeth-er in the comfort of shade trees or in the local pool hall. One dilapidated pool table sits outside a shop where several Taita men pass around warped cue sticks and haggle over the rules. From my vantage point, I believe the eight ball is missing.

I would expect villagers to have back problems, but that does not seem to be the case. Actually, everyone here is very strong and physically fit. They do not need to find a gym or spa. I believe that most of their medical problems revolve around fighting infections and healing broken bones.

Hiking on Mount Kasigau to photograph the wildlife provides us a change of pace from our daily chores. Gabri-el takes us to the source of the spring. Water trickles down the mountain over rocks laden with goat, cow, and baboon dung onto the collection point in the village. This water is also for bathing. Jasmine carries containers up several steps to a drum tank that feeds our outhouse shower. She is so strong.

One day, Jasmine's young son guides us to the spot where we can examine the 'foot of Jesus' imprinted on a rock. He tells us, "This happened when Jesus resurrected and he put a foot down on each continent before going to heaven." Indeed, we do see the shape of a large footprint, approximately twelve by twenty-four inches, fossilized in the rock.

Some days I ride through the village on a local bicy-cle called a black mamba, named after one of the deadliest snakes in Kenya. Hateb makes sure the tires always have air in case I want to jump on and take a ride.

The days run together. I have been having nightmares every night. Is it the Malarone, the antimalarial agent used to prevent malaria infections, that I am taking? Last night I had three dreams that Aaron betrayed me. In the one that I can remember with great clarity, he was bristling with a secret he could hardly wait to share with me. He said he had found a new exciting woman. In my dream, as I stared into space I reluctantly said, "I'm happy for you." I want to think that the paper-thin mattress is to blame and that the dream is not some kind of omen. I talk Aaron into ordering a new one from the largest open-air shop in the village. Grace, the owner, carries the mattress up the hill to our home on her head. These Taita women are amazing.

The heat grows worse every day, and all the villagers eagerly await the rainy season. The searing heat of the afternoon leaves me frantic for relief, so with our limited water supply, I wet a bath towel and spread it over my body. It dries in minutes.

At dusk one evening, I can see 'rainmakers' dancing on the horizon. At dark, I realize they are just brushfires burning on the plains in the distance. Lying in bed at night, I sometimes hear the gods rumbling in the sky, but still no rain. A flashlight shows me that the ecosystem in the grass roof over my head is teeming with life also searching for water.

My skin is parched, resembling the earth with cracks and meandering lines. My blistered lips match the dry, wrinkled leaves on the acacia trees. The road in and out of Rukanga is a whirling dervish of fine red dust that engulfs the vehicles and nests in my nose, mouth, and scalp.

One evening as we dine with Hateb and his family at their home, a few sprinkles fall from the sky. Hateb relays his praises: "As guests, you have brought the rain with you. Now we are all blessed. Thank you." *Imagine that, us and rain?* It's a charming belief.

Aaron and I have spent six weeks in the bush and desperately need a change of scenery. I suggest we go to Mombasa on the Indian Ocean for the weekend. We have no idea how we will get there but we will.

The Short Rains

You could feel the rain before it came, the signals were that good.

—Rod McKuen in "Cry of the Kalahari"

A Sea Breeze

There is no foreign land; it is the traveller only that is
foreign

—Robert Louis Stevenson

October 2003
Mombasa, Kenya

Aaron and I prepare well for our trip to Mombasa or at least we think we do. This is a first for us. We miss the 9:00 a.m. matatu because we sleep in after being up so late packing. Now we have to wait in the heat until 11:30 a.m. I just want to feel some air that has moisture in it and to see water. After the thirty-five-kilometer ride through the dust bowl, we arrive in Maungu wrapped in the red stuff.

We watch for busses coming from Nairobi headed in the direction of Mombasa. I think it's best for me to be the one to give the universal hitchhiking sign, and Aaron agrees. He stays in the shadows of a wood-carving shop. I can only imagine how I look standing along the main road, a for-eigner, with my thumb held high. Several busses pass, and I'm elated when one comes to a stop.

The driver looking amazed quizzes me. "Where are you headed?"

"Mombasa. Do you have room for my friend and I?"

"I'm so sorry, but we are full today. Try the next bus that comes by."

I try again. I really want a nice bus, but we get what we get.

This is a country of public transportation, with so many busses on the highway. Many of them crash and burn because of overcrowding, high speeds, potholed roads, poor shocks, and tired or drugged drivers. Hence, busses here are called "coffins on wheels."

One finally gives us a lift. A nice gentleman in the front offers up his seat for me and moves farther back. Aaron sits on the floor by the bus driver so that we don't have to be separated. Later, we learn that the Coast Bus takes reservations and we could have reserved seats at their office in Voi and avoided the hitchhiking episode, but then we would have "missed the dance."

From what we can gather, the Chinese built the section of highway from Nairobi to Voi. It's like a beautiful country road you might find in the United States. Kenyans were given an equal amount of money to build the remaining section from Voi to Mombasa, which is an incomplete road full of crater-like holes and rough, broken shoulders. Per the locals, this is a prime example of government corruption at its worst.

As I gaze out the handprint smeared window, I occasionally detect a policeman or two standing along the roadway. They are in the middle of nowhere without a car or shelter. The gentleman sitting next to me must see the perplexed look on my face because he explains, "They can wave a vehicle over to check on licenses and insurance, but they have no means to chase down an offender. Actually, they are driven out to their site along the road at sunrise, left there for the day, picked up at the end of their shift at dusk, and then taken to the local police barracks for the night. Most make extra money in the form of bribes accepted in exchange for not writing a ticket; therefore, these jobs are in high demand and someone must know someone to get hired." I'm amazed at how sharply they are dressed for this roadside post, and I refuse to believe they are all corrupt.

An occasional giraffe, zebra, or warthog can be viewed grazing in the open fields or along the shoulder of the road. I laugh at the baboon families that congregate in the middle of the road looking for a handout.

Near the villages, people galore walk to and fro. I believe many do simply because they cannot afford public transportation. I'm amazed to see Kenyans, who are in dust and heat all day, tirelessly working to keep themselves and their clothing clean. We cross scant streams, and see people washing clothes and even an occasional car. I admire their commitment to this higher order.

Our arrival into the hustle and bustle of Mombasa, a massive urban center loud with vehicles and crowded with people, is a shock. Vendors try to sell their wares including bananas, fruit juices, and nuts by shoving them through the open windows of our bus. I'm overwhelmed and want to head back into the bush.

Heather told us the Lotus Hotel is where all the Peace Corps workers stay because it is UN-security approved. But how will we find it? Another kind gentleman on the bus hears our concerns and offers to lead the way. Walk, jump on a matatu, walk again. We have trouble keeping up with him, but eventually we are close, and he points the way to the hotel. Thank you.

We take showers and walk to a shopping area in search of fabrics. I plan to hang large amounts of fabric in our banda to create a ceiling that can catch all the critter droppings from our grass roof. I remember seeing colorful print fabrics of Aboriginal designs hanging, for ambience I suppose, in one of my favorite restaurants in Nashville. I want to duplicate the look, mainly for purposes of functionality, but what a cool eclectic touch it will bring to our new environment. The market has the finest selection of prints and I'm thrilled to choose the perfect designs for the project. Yeah.

On Saturday we share breakfast in the hotel and then shop for pillows in the Elephant Tusk area of town. Next, we plan our escape to the South Coast and the Indian Ocean. We have to cross the channel via the Likoni Ferry, the one that sank a few years back with hundreds of victims drowning.

Today a multitude of passengers stand on the sidewalk, waiting for the cars to load so they can board. Many women carry huge burdens on their heads, like sacks of vegetables. Some men have homemade, wooden-wheeled carts full of items. I imagine all these items will end up at the beach resorts. The pedestrian passengers crowd onto the upper deck. I'm so glad we hired a taxi to take us all the way to the coast resorts of Diani. Before we even exit the ferry, I can smell the sea but am disappointed that the hotel we had planned to stay at is closed. Tourism is still suffering from the 1998 bombing of the Kenyan and Tanzanian embassies.

The Leisure Lodge becomes our new destination, and it is a tropical paradise. We are here all the way from the dry savannahs of Tsavo to the humid tropical landscape. The sea is clear aquamarine. The palm trees are heavy with fresh vegetation. The white sand is like baby powder, and the warm water is a luxury. We stroll along the beach and splash in the surf for hours.

We meet a couple out on the veranda. He's from the island of Lamu, and she's from Italy. They appear to be very much in love, laughing and holding hands. He tells us of the wonderful island that's his home off the northern part of Kenya's coast, and now it's on my list. She explains that they spend six months out of the year in Italy and the other six months here. I like that idea. We see many other similar couples, and I quickly find out that the coast resorts are a playground for Europeans on holidays.

Dinner is served in a beautiful garden atrium, but when we approach, we are declined entry because Aaron is not wearing long pants. We return to the room for Aaron to change clothes, but he has not packed any long pants. We eat dinner in our room and watch the local news and a foreign soap opera on the first TV we have seen since arriving in Kenya. As I relax on the bed, Aaron, sorting through his luggage, mentions that he's low on his seizure meds. This heightens my stress as I think about the logistics for our return to Rukanga. We do not have a plan in place, and even if we did, we may very well encounter unexpected delays. I'm concerned for his health and safety and worry about what I'll do if he should have a seizure. These thoughts consume me but Aaron assures me that he will be fine not to worry. Easy for him to say.

Before leaving Idaho, I met a man who said that his daughter is living and working in Mombasa. I have her phone number and decide to give her a call. Lynn graciously invites us to come visit on Sunday. We arrive just as she's setting a lunch table on the patio overlooking the ocean. We spend the early afternoon on the beach with Lynn, her husband, Paul, and their two small children. Both Lynn and Paul are working for the United States Agency for International Development (USAID) and have been living outside of the U.S. for the past seven years. Paul shares that he and Malachite work on several projects to assist the local Taita communities in sustainable agriculture, including the development of fish ponds and finding ways to entice honey bees to recolonize the area. What a coincidence that we have connected so far from home.

It's been comforting to meet these kindred spirits. When it's time for us to get back on the road, we say our goodbyes and are happy for their invitation to come back anytime. *Thank you. We will.*

Our taxi driver recommends we take the Virgin Islands bus back to the bush. He drops us off in a sea of busses, taxis, and matatus. We're at another staging area, and drivers are yelling out for customers. Prospective riders are milling about and haggling over prices. We wander through the chaos. Our backpacks are heavy and our suitcases full. Where is the Virgin Islands bus? We must watch our step, for some of the busses are leaving and others are arriving. At last I spot a bright yellow bus with palm trees painted on the sides. It's relatively small, in comparison with the Coast Bus, dilapidated and overcrowded.

The driver puts all our goods on top. We are returning with important supplies: medicines, bottled water, canned tuna, coffee, powered creamer, books, and world news. On the bus, live chickens brush up against our ankles and tickle us, ducks quack loudly as they roam under the rickety seats. I guess they will be someone's dinner tonight. The trip is long in the darkness. We arrive around nine o'clock and are actually grateful to be back in the bush.

Biking for Conservation

There is religion in everything around us, a calm and holy religion in the unbreathing things in nature.

—John Ruskin

October 2003
Mount Kasigau, Kenya

Watching the sun set every night and come up over the mountain every morning is an important ritual here for us. On a clear day, we might get a glimpse of Mount Kilimanjaro. Even so, life in the bush gets wearisome quickly once we are back from the ocean.

We feel a shift in how we are perceived and how we might contribute to projects here in Kenya. I believe word of our connection to Lynn and Paul of USAID has been shared with the community partners who are striving for successful outcomes on their projects.

Today we are scheduled to meet with the Taita Chief. He gives us a tour of his office and the food storage area for the five Kasigau communities. The area is guarded twenty-four seven. Much of the grain inside is made up of donations from agencies similar to USAID. The food will be distributed as needed during drought conditions, which to my mind are already here.

The Taita Chief and his committee invite us to help plan a Biking for Conservation event that the chief has been dreaming about for several years. He believes it's of great importance to protect the natural resources in the area and address the human/wildlife conflicts that continue to sabotage the efforts. Opting to advance his goals and objectives through a sporting challenge that will be educational and engaging, he is thrilled to express his enthusiasm, "This year my vision is becoming a reality thanks to many volunteers from the Kasigau Conservation Trust, TDC, and other supporters and donors."

We share his excitement and are happy to join the effort. Categories for the event include men eighteen to forty-nine years of age, women, and senior men fifty and up. Aaron will film, and I'll write an article for the *Kasigau Conservationist* and *SWARA*, a monthly magazine that is the voice of conservation for East Africa. In the evening we light a candle and I set up the newsletter on Microsoft Publisher. I feel like I have finally accomplished something thanks to Derek, my youngest son, who located the correct fire wire in the U.S. and sent it here so our digital devices can share information.

*

TDC staff has been picking us up on a more consistent basis. For me, the real highlights of going to TDC are the morning and afternoon game drives. Encountering the Tsavo lions is a special occurrence. The lions are descendants of the two famous man-eating lions responsible for killing an undetermined number of Indians who worked on the Nairobi–Mombasa railway in the late 1800s. The males do not have the furry manes like their brothers in other parts of Africa, and they do their own hunting instead of relying on the female of the species to hunt for them. No one is certain why male Tsavo lions have no mane, but it may be an adaptation to thick bush where long hair is a liability. A bigger question is: Why do they do their own hunting, and why did two of them develop a taste for humans?

On today's trip, as the sun is setting, I spot two lions at the watering hole, a male and female. They do not appear to be upset with our approach. Then suddenly, the female rises, looks directly at me, and saunters off into the bush. Her body is covered by fur so short she almost looks hairless. I video her strong powerful stride and key in on her large padded feet that are reddish like the soil. She exits my sights, sporting an inner confidence that she is Queen of the Jungle. Tsavo is known as an arid region with fine red soils, and when the wind howls, it whips up a substantial dust storm. We already have the soil in our clothes and our hair. And we have the stains on our feet just like the lioness.

I'm honored when Leigh asks if I would like to interview Bruce Patterson, a zoologist from the Chicago Field Museum who spends much of his time in the Tsavo area studying these handsome lions. I find Bruce relaxing at his African research site in Galla Camp. Bruce is happy to do an interview to promote his project in this area and his upcoming book *Lions of Tsavo.*

"I come here at least twice a year with a group of volunteers from around the world who support Earth Watch," he says. "The data we are recording will be invaluable for determining the longevity of the species." He smiles before continuing. "I'm not related to the famous Lt. Colonel John Henry Patterson, who was able to track and kill the two Tsavo lions that caused such loss of life during the building of a bridge over the Tsavo River for the railroad."

"Don't you have those two lions mounted and displayed at your museum?" I ask. "I believe I've seen those on one of my trips to Chicago."

"Yes, they are in the Rice Gallery and are two of the most famous residents."

I thank Bruce Patterson for his time and let him know that his story will be featured in our first edition of the conservation newsletter that goes to publication in January. When Bruce and the Earth Watch volunteers head home, TDC staff with volunteers will continue to count and collect data on the Tsavo lions. Working with such interesting people and their projects is energizing me, and I can't wait to share the stories with those back home.

After the awesome interview, Aaron realizes he forgot to bring meds with us to TDC. The only solution is to go back to Voi to catch a matatu to Rukanga. It takes him all afternoon. In the evening, Leigh radios ahead, "There has been an incident. You need to be available to care for Aaron when he returns to TDC."

"What kind of incident?" I ask. But Leigh is already off the shortwave radio.

I don't know if he has been in a car accident or has had a seizure. I'm really worried. He returns at dark with his forehead bandaged. As we sit on the bed holding hands, Aaron shares his harrowing experience:

"When I got to the banda, I reached in my pocket. What the hell? No key. I yelled for Williamson or Hateb. I was burning up, so I jumped into the shower. Next thing I know I'm all wet sitting on the slimy floor. Blood is dripping from my forehead. I head down to the village and run into a woman who bandages my forehead. Finally, Hateb comes running with the key, and I get the meds. Then it's a matatu ride back to Voi where I run into Leigh, and he calls you on our way back here."

"I'm so sorry I didn't go with you."

Aaron climbs under the covers, and I forego the evening game drive to stay with him.

The next day is also taxing, as we have to get a ride to Voi and then catch a ride back to Rukanga. At least I'm able to solicit some gift certificates for mosquito nets from the local shops. These will be given as prizes for the upcoming bike derby in December. The Trust is promoting the use of mosquito nets to help reduce the incidences of malaria, especially in children.

At dusk we get the last matatu of the evening. Our matatu has no headlights. The driver and his helper use our wide-beam flashlight to navigate the harrowing roads. Nightjars, nocturnal birds who have a habit of resting and/ or roosting on roads, flutter in front of us as we proceed slowly back into the bush.

An Unwelcome Visitor

When your heart speaks, take good notes.

—Judith Campbell

October 2003
Voi, Kenya

O n the way to TDC a week later, Aaron tells me that we will have no money for the next fourteen to twenty-one days, according to his financial advisor back home. In desperation I share this with Sammy, the TDC kitchen manager, and he offers to take us to the bank in Voi so that we can set up an account and perhaps take out a loan. When we arrive in Voi, I'm so excited to see an ATM machine at the bank entrance.

"Aaron, there's an ATM machine. Use your debit card and we can get some cash and won't have to wait for Western Union."

"I don't have a debit card," Aaron says, as if he doesn't even know what that is.

I try to bite my tongue but cannot help myself. "You don't have a debit card?"

Aaron just shrugs his shoulders, which leaves me exasperated.

Sammy introduces us to the bank manager, and an account is set up for us.

Now we have a bank account but with a zero balance. Aaron tries valiantly to seduce the loan officer, but she denies us even a small advance.

When I see Malachite in a meeting at the chief's office the following day, I embarrassingly ask, "Would you happen to have a few extra shillings that I might borrow for dinner tonight. I know this is strange for an American asking a Kenyan for money, but..."

He hands me 3,000 shillings, enough for several dinners. Then he makes me laugh.

"I know that Westerners can also have troubles, but they do not wear them on their sleeves like Africans, who do not hesitate to give detailed accounts of their hard-luck stories."

"Thank you, Malachite. I really appreciate this, and I promise to pay you back as soon as we get money from the states." He smiles.

Now I'm beholden to another man.

All of this stress is taking its toll on me, and after two months in the bush, I wake up early on the morning of my birthday and feel really sick, like I might have a urinary tract infection. I have pain in my lower back. I had an infection once before when I was in college, and I recognize the symptoms. I'm beside myself. I have suffered from anxiety and panic attacks most of my life, but they are elevated here in a developing country. The village doesn't have a doctor, and we have no vehicle to drive to Voi. Suddenly, the severity of living in the bush in Africa is revealed.

Aaron finds me sobbing.

He wraps his arms around me. "Honey, I'm going to get someone from the village to help us."

I'm left alone and depressed. Beginning a new life in a new country with a new man isn't as simple or as romantic as it seemed that day at the lake when we made our decision to spend a year in Africa.

Aaron returns with Heather, a welcome sight.

She brings Ciprofloxacin, an antibiotic that treats a variety of bacterial infections. "Take 500 milligrams two times a day for the next five days," she says.

We hug, and I say a heartfelt, "Thanks."

I feel better immediately and ask Aaron to walk with me to one of my favorite places, Guy Rock. I can breathe here, and my anxiety begins to subside.

"I don't feel grounded here in Kenya. Something is missing and out of balance."

I blurt this out as I watch the falcons circle before they disappear behind the shadows of a cliff.

"What do you want?" Aaron asks.

"I want my freedom back. I want to have some control over my life here."

Aaron, looking concerned and deep in thought, finally says, "Let's buy a motorbike once my money arrives."

"Yes, wheels will help us gain back some independence."

When we arrive back at our banda, we have visitors waiting for us, a common occurrence here. I serve African tea and tell them it is my birthday.

"Really, we do not celebrate birthdays," the banda manager says. "Actually, we do not even know exactly when we were born. I just know that I was born during the year of the locust."

Tempest laughingly adds, "I was born during the year of the great flood."

And Kent says, "I was born during the year of the typhoid outbreak."

Kent has brought us mail that arrived at TDC from the U.S. When I open a birthday card from my youngest son, I burst into tears. I'm embarrassed but can't hide the fact that I'm missing home. I'm also overwhelmed with the difficulties of living here. Every ordinary task is a challenge. Washing clothes by hand can take up to two hours. Preparing a well-balanced meal can take longer. You have to soak all the fresh fruits and vegetables in bleach and cook and bake one item at a time over the propane burner, and all with no refrigeration for proper storage.

Aaron and I had tried to figure out how to make a fruit cellar to at least keep items cool. We dug a deep hole in the dirt around the base of the banda on the north, the shady side. And then we placed a few green oranges, the only kind of oranges available here, at the bottom and covered them up for the night. The next morning, we checked on our experiment only to see a swarm of insects gathered.

Aaron tells Kent about our desire to be more independent. Kent says he can get us a bike from his brother in Tanzania, so Aaron promises we will pay 9000 Kenya Shillings or 100 USD when the bike arrives. This should not cause me more stress, but it does.

I have enjoyed sharing birthday stories with our new friends, and they have loved hearing about how we celebrate birthdays. Each one wishes me a happy birthday and departs in the afternoon heat.

In the evening, Heather is back with a birthday cake she has baked on her propane burner in the village. It is chocolate with chocolate icing, my favorite. *How did she do it?* I'm overwhelmed with her kindness. We light candles, sing "Happy Birthday," and give thanks for our incredible lives.

Heather and I confer about what we miss the most living out here. It's not our favorite foods or plumbing and electricity. It's our freedom: freedom to get in a car and drive to where we want to go and freedom to pick up a phone and call whomever we want. But we also miss something that's a given back home but a luxury in the savannah, ice.

She leaves after dark, and Aaron walks her down the path. I sit in silence. Why am I feeling trapped in this beautiful land? I have come so far as a woman, and now I have put myself back in time. I'm completely dependent upon a man for my existence which is the very thing my mother fought so diligently to overcome. She worked hard to make sure I received a college education; she wanted me to be an independent woman.

I was tested in my marriage as an addiction took my husband hostage. When it tightened its grip on him, I juggled two jobs, took over the majority of parenting our two sons, kept the checkbook balanced, maintained our guise as a normal happy couple, and even hid the details from my immediate family.

On the verge of a physical, mental, and emotional avalanche, I reached out to a therapist. She informed me that I was enabling my husband to continue his addiction by taking over all the family responsibilities. This is why I had exhausted myself to the point of near collapse. Then she asked, "How do you envision your relationship with your husband?"

"I see us out in the middle of a lake. I'm treading water while he's struggling to stay afloat. He's reaching for me."

"And?"

"He's going to pull me under."

"Tell you husband that you're sorry but you cannot save him. Then turn and swim to shore."

I said I was sorry and swam to shore.

Sounds so simple. I wish it could have been, but it wasn't. This was the beginning of months of hard work that started with an intervention that led to his two failed attempts at rehabilitation and culminated in separation and, ultimately, divorce.

I accepted Aaron's offer to finance this adventure as a gift, a gift which I greatly appreciate, but financial insecurity has become a nagging distraction from the life I envisioned.

Tonight's *Malarone Dream:*

I am a "spy" and working with a male with the Code name "BLUE." We have a brief sexual encounter, and then he goes off into the deepest part of the jungle. Sometime much later, I hear voices and see a procession of people approaching across the savannah towards me. Some are singing and some are playing musical instruments. I realize it is a funeral procession. When they get close, I ask what this is all about. The spokesperson states that BLUE died in the jungle. It appears that he must not have any immediate family since they have come to me and I only had a brief encounter with him. I ask how he died, and they say that he died of starvation waiting for his funds to arrive.

I awake startled.

When the bike arrives two weeks later, we find that it's not safe for riding. Both the frame and the wheels are badly out of alignment. Aaron has received funds from home and pays the 9000 ksh. I'm pissed off. Something has to change...

A Snake Encounter

To live in Africa, you must know
what it's like to die in Africa.

—Ernest Hemingway

November 2003
Mount Kasigau, Kenya

A aron has taken a matatu to Voi town for another wire transfer, and I'm left alone with Jasmine, washing clothes and cleaning the lizard droppings from our living quarters; our fabric ceiling is not a catch-all. The mid-morning temperature is pleasant compared to yesterday's overbearing heat. Jasmine sings as she works, and I hang the freshly washed clothing on the line.

All is well until I hear her bloodcurdling scream, "Snake, snake."

She comes running out of the bedroom and into the yard. I run down the hill towards the village to find Hateb. He has heard the screams and is flying up the path. Jasmine and Hateb chase the snake down and fight it off by spraying Raid, while I stand frozen in place at the front door. I can hear the spray, and then Hateb and Jasmine stagger out of the room, coughing and gagging. They are overpowering the snake with its own weapon of spitting.

Ten minutes of this goes on, and I'm still in shock. Later, Jasmine carries the snake out on a stick and sets it on a rock. Hateb franticly beats the snake. I plead, "Stop, stop. It's dead," but I'm told that the snake might just be playing dead.

When the village elders arrive, they confirm that it is a venomous red spitting cobra.

It's getting late, and Aaron is still in Voi on business. I remember that Aaron had laser surgery on his eyes before our trip because he wanted to be able to spot a snake in the night without having to reach for his glasses. Now I'm afraid to go to bed. Many times in the past I heard strange noises when I would walk into the bedroom. I'm convinced that if there's one snake there must be another. One of our security guards, sweet Williamson, tells me he would sleep in the banda to protect me if he could, but he must sleep in the shed outside since rules are rules. I understand.

I just finished reading Hemingway's final novel, *True at First Light*, written when he returned from his 1953 safari and edited by his son Patrick after his death. It is a rich blend of autobiography and fiction. It passionately details the African landscape, the thrill of the hunt, and the heartfelt relationships with his African neighbors, the Maasai. In it, he is convinced that snakes are the ancestors of all the Maasai. He thought the coldness of the Maasai women's hands and the occasional coldness of other parts of their bodies could be because of snake blood.

I have another Malarone dream:

Ernest Hemmingway stands in my foyer, picking me up for our date. He wears a brown leather jacket with blue pants that are nicely pressed with a crease but a little baggy. His hair is dark and slicked back. I am surprised at the difference in our ages. He is much older. He has a limp, and I remember he was in an airplane accident in Kenya. I ask him to wait five minutes while I run upstairs to retrieve the house keys. I look in all the drawers. No luck.

After ten minutes I go back to him and apologize for the delay and he says, "No problem, I went to see a movie while I was waiting."

"How could you see a movie in ten minutes?" I ask.

He explains that the day before he had missed the first ten minutes of a particular film and now had a chance to see it. I wrap my arm through his, and off we slip into the night.

At first light, Aaron arrives and wakes me. I shout, "Hey, I was on a date with Hemingway and now I don't know where he was taking me!"

Once fully awake, reality sinks in, and I shudder telling Aaron about the snake. Of course, he wants to see it, so I take him to where it is still draped over a large rock with its head and tail dangling over the sides. Still traumatized, I fear it might come back to life any minute. I rush back into the banda, dragging Aaron with me. We hold each other close for the longest time.

Unstable Air

*The use of traveling is to regulate imagination by
reality, and instead of thinking how things may be, to
see them as they are.*

—Samuel Johnson

November 2003
Nairobi, Kenya

W ord spreads quickly through the village and all the
way to Voi town about the snake incident. Weldon
from the East African Wildlife Society (EAWLS) shows up on
our doorstep and invites us to go to Nairobi. He must recognize the need for us to get out of the bush. We toss some
clothes in our backpacks and leave for Nairobi. When we
pass Cobra Rock on the way to the main highway, I flinch.
Weldon encourages me to relax. He will become, like Pooh
Bear says, a forever friend but for now there are more lessons to be learned about time in Africa.

Our first stop is to see Rob, an Aussie who lives in
Kenya. He is the operations director for the Canadian
owner of Rukinga Ranch. We are picking up a friend of
his and giving him a lift to Nairobi. Empty Tusker beer

cans frame the entrance to Rob's new house. Rob and his friends are just waking, and they all have hangovers. Alexandra, a twenty-something, comes staggering out of a bedroom. She is covered with colorful tattoos from her neck to her toes. My muscles tense. We learn she is from Texas. Her wealthy father has sent her here in hopes that she will grow up.

My mind wonders. I like this house. It has character. A hand-carved wooden bench and a wicker console with matching mirror rest on the colorful ceramic tile floor. Beaded artwork hangs on the walls. I can imagine myself living in a place like this.

We finally get underway and arrive in Voi around 11:00 a.m. We are picking up Malachite. When he shows up, I get his version of an English greeting: a kiss on both cheeks and a final kiss on the lips.

Is this normal for here? No one else I have met does this.

Obviously, Malachite has adopted some of the European rituals but adds his own creative adaptations. He is handsome, looks younger than his forty-something years, and is charming. He has a coyness about him that attracts me.

We are delayed while Malachite completes some office work. Aaron and I run errands and pick up cash from Western Union. It is past noon when we attempt to depart for Nairobi once again. I'm ready for lunch but there is no mention of this luxury.

Our adventure continues to the Kenya Wildlife Service (KWS) Headquarters in Tsavo West National Park. Weldon seems to enjoy driving like a maniac down the Nairobi–Mombasa highway, all while speaking endlessly on his new mobile phone. When we arrive, I need to find a bathroom. Malachite grabs my hand and leads me to the facilities. I slip 3000 ksh into his hand to pay back what I had borrowed from him a few weeks ago. He smiles and whispers in my ear, *Thank you*. I wonder if Aaron is watching, and if so, I wonder what he is thinking.

Malachite plans to introduce me to the Deputy Warden. I will discuss giving a Certified Interpretive Guide (CIG) training course to his staff. This is the same training I have provided our summer rangers back home. I carry a proposal with me. While I'm waiting, I read the KWS Mission statement:

We hold in trust, for now and tomorrow, the responsibility for protection and conservation of Kenya's extraordinary wealth, as represented by its fauna, flora and natural beauty. KWS will manage these resources, which are of inestimable economic, socio-cultural, aesthetic and scientific value. To fulfill this mission KWS will develop the required human resources, achieve financial self-sufficiency and encourage support and participation of the people of Kenya.

Then I read the unofficial motto listed below:

We the willing, led by the unknowing, are doing the impossible for the ungrateful. We have done so much for so long with so little, we are now qualified to do anything with nothing.

I'm amused because I believe this is also an unofficial motto of many U.S. government agencies. The warden arrives and invites me into his office. I'm grateful to have a chance to tell him about NAI:

NAI defines interpretation as "a mission-based communication process that forges emotional and intellectual connections between the interests of the audience and the meanings inherent in the resource." Interpreters connect visitors to important natural, cultural, and historical resources at parks, nature centers, historical sites, aquariums, zoos, and anywhere that people come to learn about places.

The thirty-two–hour CIG training includes:
- history, definition, and principles of interpretation
- making your programs purposeful, enjoyable, relevant, organized, and thematic
- using tangible objects to connect audiences to intangible ideas and universal concepts in interpretive programs
- presentation and communication skills
- certification requirements (fifty-question literature review; program outline; a twenty-to-thirty-minute presentation)

He listens politely but makes no commitment. As we attempt to leave an hour later, our Land Rover door is jammed and now another delay. I believe our Kenyan colleagues are on friendly terms with time. They seem to be enjoying the delays, while Aaron and I find them annoying. I remind myself that patience is a virtue.

Finally, the door is fixed and we are on our way again. Weldon continues to drive at breakneck speed. Watching oncoming traffic scares me, so I close my eyes and try to sleep. I'm sitting in the back seat between Malachite and Aaron. Their thighs press against mine. I don't want to think, and I certainly don't want to feel either, but the thighs are attached to two handsome men.

I learn that Malachite is the name of a gemstone referred to as the "stone of transformation." The stone assists one in changing situations and achieving spiritual growth.

So perhaps I should not block what it is that he is bringing to me…

The car continues on its course, barreling around sharp curves and swerving to dodge potholes in the road. The changing motion throws each man against my body, alternately.

Now I can't help but wonder what it would be like to share a bed with both of these men at the same time.

Slightly outside of Nairobi, we arrive at Weldon's sister's house, where we will stay. I find out that Lena works for the government in the health care field. She is the most gracious host. Malachite will continue on to Nairobi, where he will stay with his family. Before he takes leave, I see Aaron motion for him to come into the backyard. They get pretty far from me, and I can't tell for sure what is going on. I watch intently, and it looks as if they are having a heated discussion. A few minutes later, Malachite quickly departs.

Later in the evening I spy a litter of kittens as they play on the back porch. One of the kittens takes a liking to me. I ask if I might adopt this little sweetheart. She has no name, so I suggest, Kasi, short for Kasigau. It's a done deal; she is ours. Weldon says, "She will alert you to any critters in the banda like snakes."

Everyone assumes Aaron and I are married. At bedtime, I plant a tender goodnight kiss on Aaron's cheek and ask, "What were you and Malachite discussing in the back yard earlier tonight?"

"I told him that you belong to me so back off."

In a way I'm flattered. In another way I want to say, *I'm not your property.* I keep silent and turn over with my back to Aaron, waiting for sleep to come.

Learning Africa

Like the river, we were free to wander.

—Aldo Leopold

November 2003
Nairobi, Kenya

B reakfast is ready when we arise, and then we are off for town. Weldon tells us we will be using Lena's car, a 1990 Honda sedan, while they both report for work.

Aaron and I meet the challenge of driving for the first time in a country that drives on the left side of the road. We take turns at the wheel. The car has a manual transmission, and I haven't operated a stick shift since learning to drive when I was fifteen. We dodge pedestrians dressed in colorful attire, cyclists wandering in and out of traffic, matatus blaring their music, trucks honking their horns, and overloaded busses speeding past. Most intersections are roundabouts with no traffic lights or yield signs. Navigating through them is my biggest stressor.

Weldon introduces us to the entire staff at the EAWLS office. Malachite is a most accommodating host, but remains a bit reserved with me today. He only kisses me on the cheeks. Before heading out on errands, we are invited to a lunch of scrumptious beef stew, cornbread, and banana fritters. *Thank you.*

Once on the road I catch a glimpse of a sign for Nairobi National Park. I have heard that the Sheldrick Wildlife Trust, which takes in orphaned baby elephants and reintroduces them into the wild, is operating within the park boundaries. We manage to make our way through all the gates and guards and end up on Daphne Sheldrick's doorstep. She is sitting on the front porch with some associates and gives us a warm welcome. I explain that we have come to adopt/sponsor a baby elephant. The baby elephants are from four months to ten months old. Daphne gives us permission to walk out on the savannah and meet up with the orphans being brought into the yard for their daily mud bath. They are so playful. One baby comes directly over to me and studies me with his trunk. His name is Taita. What a perfect baby to adopt. Daphne tells us that Taita was found in the Taita Hills area. He had fallen into an open well and was struggling to survive when the villagers found him and sought help. Most of the babies are named for the areas in which they were found. Before we leave, we watch Taita get his baby blanket put over his back, drink his milk from a large baby bottle, and go with his surrogate mother, a trainer, for a nap. What fun.

Aaron wants to purchase a video projector so that we can share our encounters with wildlife such as this current interaction. Many school-age children in and around the suburbs of Nairobi, and even around Mount Kasigau, have never had the opportunity to go on a game drive. We find an electronics store and negotiate a sale. While we are waiting to finalize the purchase, I catch breaking news on a TV screen. The British Embassy in Istanbul has been bombed. President George W. Bush is in London meeting with Tony Blair as Londoners and people in other parts of the world are protesting the Iraq War. I suddenly feel vulnerable being in a foreign country.

In many places we are called "ugly Americans." I attempt to separate myself from those thoughts. I reach for the projector and imagine the fun I'm going to have introducing baby Taita to the children in our new community.

When we pick up Weldon and his sister in the afternoon, we find out that the matatu drivers are going on strike tomorrow because the President and his Safety Commission have declared that all matatus must have seatbelts for all passengers. This will be a major problem for owners and drivers. Most vans will only be able to carry fourteen passengers instead of the twenty plus they usually pile in. Installing seatbelts will be expensive, and then the income will decrease. Matatus are privately owned and operated vans that add enormously to the chaos on the roads. The drivers are usually young men, and they are paid by the number of passengers they transport. Loud music, flashing neon lights, kaleidoscopic paint jobs, and trendy names like *No Nonsense* and *The Survivors* attract riders. Passengers are herded in like cattle by the recruiter, who encourages additional riders to hang from the roof, windows, or open doors. The matatu driver doesn't move until the vehicle is sufficiently overloaded. Neither the owner nor the driver is held responsible for passenger safety. The Kenyan newspapers *The Nation* and *The Standard* have reported horrific stories of matatus crashing and passengers being injured or worse.

But this day, large crowds mill around the main square, waiting for still-running matatus to transport them home from the market. They stand in endless queues, arms loaded with plastic bags full of daily necessities. Children run barefoot through the stalled traffic, some selling items, some begging, and others just playing with toy cars.

*

S trike day is here. Army soldiers patrol the streets. Some are wearing riot gear.

People drive their personal vehicles, and we encounter horrific traffic jams. This provides beggars the opportunity to weave their way through the jumble of cars to knock on windows and ask for shillings. Many sell magazines, sunglasses, cosmetics, or whatever they think you might need or buy. There is always someone leading a blind person through the maze.

We enjoy morning tea with the EAWLS staff and purchase sweatshirts from the gift shop to keep us warm in the cool rain. Then Aaron receives $15,000 from home through Western Union. What?

I'm so excited, "Can we buy a car?"

"You want a car?"

"Yes. Don't you?"

"Okay. Let's get one. It will be fun."

"We are experienced drivers now, and just think, no more matatus." *Hooray.*

But for the moment we are still driving the borrowed Honda. Exhausted at the end of the day, we have to find our way back to EAWLS. We get lost looking for River Road and then find ourselves in yet another major traffic jam. I suggest we pull into the first parking space we see. Cell phones are a relatively new commodity in Kenya, and texting is much cheaper than calling, so I text Weldon: *SOS, we are stranded.*

He replies, *Wait and I will come in a company car to get you.*

We wait two hours. He is caught in a similar traffic jam. When he arrives, we follow him two blocks to Kenyatta Avenue, which takes another hour. There we sit in the middle of the intersection with everyone maneuvering to get through. I have only seen traffic jams like this in movies. Some people get out of their cars and try to get others to back up or pull forward so they can get around. Weldon warns, "Someone may run up to us and try to steal our jewelry or watches or our phones right off of us," so we have to keep all our windows shut even though we have an open can of gas in the back.

Finally, we are able to edge our way out of town.

We agree that maybe the matatus drivers have won this round, but the government has said it will not back down. Seat belts and speed governors must be installed by January 2nd.

In all this chaos, I have spotted a shiny white Land Cruiser with a FOR SALE sign. Land Cruisers are known to be the best vehicles for off-road excursions. This may be our lucky day after all. I quickly call the number displayed. An American woman owns the car. She purchased it from the Norwegian Embassy.

The next day the vehicle is brought to the EAWLS office. It doesn't look as good as it did yesterday, but we buy it for $12,000 because it has been maintained at the embassy. Plus, the thought of returning to the village of Rukanga without a means of transportation is frightening. The driver asks if Aaron or I want to test-drive the car. Aaron says no. I say yes. I don't want Aaron buying a car that I won't be able to drive. I take over at the wheel and already love the car.

Next, we meet Ashley, the owner, at the New Stanley Hotel in downtown Nairobi to finalize the deal. She is here in Kenya working on her doctorate. I'm surprised when I find out she is documenting a cultural tradition of the Taita tribe.

"One very unique aspect of Taita culture is the respect accorded to the dead," she says. "In the past when a person died, they were buried for a period of about one year, at which time their body would be exhumed. The skull would be severed from the rest of the body and taken to a sacred cave which is their 'proper' abode with the ancestors. While this is no longer practiced, the caves where the skulls can be found are treated as sacred in many parts of the Taita Hills."

She was given permission to visit the caves surrounding the Mount Kasigau area where we are living. During the long rains last year, she was trapped in one of the villages for a month when the only road in and out flooded. What a story she has to tell.

I'm intrigued and hope I can learn more, but we need to resolve the car issue for now since she is planning to head back to the United States in a few days.

We need to get a place to stay while finalizing the car deal. The YMCA is recommended, very nice and a short walk. It turns out to be a long walk. I'm in pain from carrying a printer in my backpack along with a digital video camera and battery pack for the laptop Aaron is carrying. I also have a jar of peanut butter and some crackers, my life support system. We finally reach the Y. The place is disappointing, and I'm almost in tears. Aaron lines up a cab. The driver mentions The Fairview, and I remember the girls from Canada at TDC praising the hotel. I promise Aaron that if it's too expensive, I will reimburse him when we get home. It is a four-star place with five-star services. We have a bathtub. I'm in heaven! We are across the street from the Israeli Embassy, so we have guards at checkpoints all over the area. I even spot a soldier with a rifle up on a water tower.

We call Ashley's contact at the U.S. Embassy to finalize the deal. We are to meet tomorrow at Times Tower. *So what do we do today?* It is Ramadan and many places are closed. We decide to relax at the hotel. Dinner poolside again and we feed the host cats. Each table has a charcoal burner to add warmth. This is an incredibly romantic place.

*

Today is Thanksgiving and we spend all day at Times Tower trying to finalize the transfer of ownership of the car. African bureaucracy reacts slowly, if at all, and petty officials wield immense power. Our rep pulls some strings, and we go upstairs and acquire a PIN number. I believe a bribe just took place. We take the Land Cruiser to the Toyota dealership and find out that something may be wrong with the brakes and the steering. Another day in Nairobi is in store for us.

Aaron instructs Toyota to do all repairs per the estimate, but they tell us they have no parts. We leave the car behind, not knowing what we should do. Marabou storks along the Langata Highway watch us from high in the trees, and I bet they are laughing. Standing on average of sixty inches tall with a wingspan of eleven feet, the Marabou is one of the largest birds alive today. Once I witnessed fifty of these strange-looking birds flying over our heads and landing at a watering hole at the Voi Wildlife Lodge. A few minutes later they took off one by one; it was like being at a very busy airport.

Aaron decides that he will head out into the city alone to look for parts and I will stay behind to wash clothes and organize our stuff at the hotel. I have half of Aaron's $3,000 in my backpack. He has the other half with him. I decide that it's not a good idea to keep it all in one place, so I divide it up and put some in my suitcase.

Then, out of desperation, I do something that I'm not proud of, but I do it anyway.

I separate out $300 to keep for myself to use as an emergency fund in case I want to leave Kenya or leave Aaron.

He returns at noon and we are gone all afternoon attempting to extend our visas another ninety days. If not, we must leave the country for ten days, starting December 15. Once again, we are under the gun. The government office closes at four o'clock. We rush to procure new visa photos, which devours forty-five minutes and leaves us only five minutes to finalize our paperwork, but we manage to do it.

We return late and have dinner. Then I begin to pack. I realize that the $300 I squirreled away in the pocket of my vest is missing. I tell Aaron about the missing funds but not about my emergency exit plan. I call the front desk. The manager apologizes but reminds me of the adequate amount of signage in the lobby and in our room that says, PLACE ALL VALUABLES IN A LOCK BOX. I feel really bad about this whole state of affairs, and now we are out a considerable amount of money because of me. It is a contentious night.

*

Aaron was able to find the necessary car parts, and the car is repaired. So today we will pick it up and get our little kitten, Kasigau. In the evening, Aaron and I make plans to drive the vehicle back to Rukanga tomorrow. I can't wait to see the reactions of our Taita friends back in the bush.

Holidays Abroad

Never mind what you left behind; keep in mind what you are yet to find.

—Ghana proverb

December 2003
Mount Kasigau, Kenya

As we drive into Rukanga, all the villagers come running out to greet us as if they already knew we would be coming back in a vehicle. I'm amazed at how information floats through the air and arrives at our destination before we do. I'm driving so that the women and girls can see that it's possible for a female to drive a car. They roar, clap, and cheer me on. It's inspiring.

*

With Christmas coming soon, we head out on a trip to Mombasa for supplies and to get Kasi her shots. What a difference having a car makes; we have some control over our lives. As we approach town, we get into a round-about, and I suggest we take a left because it follows the ocean. This route feels familiar to me. We stumble upon an animal hospital inside a private residence. *Good luck!*

Dr. Fazel gives Kasi her shots and a boarding pass. He is of Indian descent and can't believe that we live in the bush. He tells us that most Africans have never lived like we are living and invites us to tea on his patio overlooking the bay. Palm trees, cool water, and calm breezes unveil a paradise in the middle of this congested city. He calls ahead and reserves a room for us at the Traveler's Beach Resort. One of his sons rides along to assist us. Check-in takes almost two hours, but when we finally get our room, we enjoy a hot shower, delicious food, and a wonderful four-poster bed.

*

A few days before Christmas, we awake excited because it is bike derby day. Through all of our ups and downs, Aaron and I have been able to meet weekly with Taita Chief Pascal and his committee to plan the event. Aaron gets his camera equipment ready, and I have pen and paper in hand since I will be writing an article for both *SWARA* and the *Kasigau Conservationist.*

We pack the gift certificates collected from local business in Voi and get Williamson, Hateb, and Jasmine to walk three bicycles down to the staging area. Aaron, extremely generous, donated the bicycles as prizes for the top three winners. EAWLS, TDC, and Rukinga Ranch have made additional donations.

We arrive at the starting line by seven. Rukanga is hosting the event, providing the staging area with the start and finish line. What we, the planners, didn't expect was such a large turnout: 137 riders show up to ride for conservation. I help with the registration along with Leigh from TDC and Rob from Rukinga Ranch.

The course circles the mountain and is nearly fifty kilometers in length. By nine, more than one thousand people are there to cheer on their favorite riders. What is heartening is not only the camaraderie I'm witnessing but how the villagers have closed off the road to all motor vehicles. Yes, matatus too.

The race begins with a wave of the Kenyan flag, and off they go. The riders have to brave the heat, the body-pounding washboard roads, and tough climbs along the way to complete the race. Many will succeed. Committee members man water stations. Weldon and Malachite run out on the course and hand plastic water bottles to those who refuse to stop even though they're thirsty.

One participant had to arise early in the morning and pedal fifty kilometers to get from Voi to the starting point in Rukanga. He collapses from dehydration and exhaustion after racing a short period of time. Heather escorts him to the nearby health clinic. He will receive the gift for having come the farthest distance to participate. Heath-er returns in time to hear the screams for the first-place winner, Kachem Kombo, two hours and fifteen minutes later.

My great honor is to present a new bicycle to the young woman, Nduku Kimeu, who takes first in the women's cate-gory. She is an inspiration not only to the women and young girls but even to the men. They are happy to congratulate her. *Amen.*

And last but not least, the audience cheers the winner of the senior men's group, Ronald Musioki. All decide on the spot that this will be an annual event.

*

T wo days before Christmas, we drive to Voi. I'm sitting in front of the Tsavo Park Hotel in the car waiting for Aaron to return from checking our mailbox, when "Joy to the World" plays loudly over a speaker, followed by "Silent Night." It is over 100 degrees. This feels so bizarre. I'm sud-denly homesick. I can see my family surrounding the light-ed Christmas tree, passing out gifts as they munch on sugar cookies and drink hot apple cider and eggnog.

I'm concerned about my eye. It appears I have some-thing embedded in the white area, and it looks red. I clear-ly remember something flying into my eye during the bike derby. Of course, I'm also sure I must have rubbed my eye at the time. Aaron reminds me that there's nothing that can be done until Friday.

Christmas comes and goes and is basically uneventful. I guess I haven't accepted responsibility for my own happiness, but New Year's will be different.

The day after Christmas we are headed back to Mombasa. My right eye is blurry and irritated. I'm holding Kasi and her newly made car carrier. Williamson made it for her, but she has already chewed her way out. We stop at Dr. Fazel's, and I ask him to recommend an eye doctor. He examines my eye and tells me it's scratched. He writes a prescription for eye drops. We sit by the ocean again and don't want to leave this hospitable environment. *Thank you, Dr. Fazel.*

When we look for a vacant room for the night, there are none to be had, so we head to Malindi, a favorite Italian destination, but when I see a sign for Watamu, I'm curious. We arrive at dusk on a very dangerous road. People are walking in the middle of the street, and various means of transportation stop and start in front of us. Families huddle around glowing embers, conversing and laughing. I'm brought back to childhood memories of sitting with my family around a campfire. I already love it here. We come across a hotel called Hemingway's. This is where Ernest Hemingway hung out on fishing expeditions, and many black and white photographs of him adorn the public areas of the resort. This place feels strangely familiar. *Is this where Ernest took me on my dream date?*

*

B efore we know New Year's Eve is upon us, and Aaron and I have created a plan for our celebration. We stay at our banda and cook African tacos with beans, onions, and tomatoes in chapatis for our dinner. I make apple crisp and it's not bad for my first attempt. We open our Christmas presents from home. Then we watch our first DVD movie on the computer, *Jurassic Park*, and use up both batteries. At midnight, we go outside to a beautiful half-moon and sing a joyful version of Auld Lang Syne. Happy New Year.

Another Malarone Dream:

I'm sitting on the front stoop of our banda at dusk. Clouds roll in over Mount Kasigau. I look up, and out of the clouds comes a single star. I prepare to see a falling star, but instead it shoots upward. I yell for Aaron to come see this phenomenon, but he keeps mumbling something that I cannot understand. I continue to watch it, and when he finally comes out, it is gone.

I'm not sure what significance this will have on my New Year's expectations, but shooting stars have guided me before.

The Dry Season

*Green fields are gone now, parched by the sun; Gone from
the valleys where rivers used to run . . .*

—Terry Gilkyson in "Cry of the Kalahari"

New Year's Resolution

*And hand in hand, on the edge of the sand, they
danced by the light of the moon.*

—Edward Lear in The Owl and the Pussycat

Winter 2004
Voi, Kenya

Aaron and I have made a New Year's Resolution: we will move to Voi town and find a place to rent that has electricity and indoor plumbing. I'm keeping my fingers crossed. We have been living in the bush since the first of September. Enough is enough. Even though we are going rogue, we still plan to continue with all of our projects from the comfort and safety of Voi town. I take it upon myself to hire Harold, an entrepreneur whom I met in Voi one day, to assist us in finding the perfect place. He is among the many who are trying to carve out a living for themselves and their families in this evolving country.

Everyone has been happy to tell us all about snakes, especially spitting cobras. When cornered, some species can spit their venom a distance as great as two meters. While spitting is typically their primary form of defense, all spitting cobras are capable of delivering venom through a bite as well. Most species' venom exhibits significant hemotoxic effects such as destroying red blood cells, disrupting blood clotting, and causing organ degeneration along with more typical neurotoxic effects such as destroying nerve tissue to the brain or spinal cord. The more I hear the more I know we have made the right decision.

After the cobra incident, we were visited by two green snakes, harmless but frightening nonetheless. They were in our grass roof one afternoon and managed to make their way down to our living area. Kasi warned me by hissing. I was trapped inside with them until Williamson chased them off. Then he climbed the tree next to the banda and chopped off the branch leaning on the roof. He suspected snakes were entering from that vantage point. Once again, I felt traumatized.

We make a recon trip to Voi and see what we think will be our new house. It has two tile bathrooms and a tile kitchen. I'm impressed. Now we will need to negotiate a price. But this is Africa (TIA), and it is always fascinating and unpredictable. Since the owner is asking 30,000 shillings a month when 10,000 to 15,000 is not only reasonable but is what Harold quoted, we leave without a contract.

The first newsletter for the Kasigau Conservation Trust is finished so we go to Ashtech and get an estimate on printing. Leigh will pick it up in a couple of days and have his staff distribute the 4000 copies. I'm pleased and proud to know we are making progress and as an added blessing, we're learning so much about Kenya and its people.

The newsletter includes: "The Chief's Corner," a "Did You Know" section, "TDC Updates," "Elephant Orphanage Highlights," "The Study of Tsavo Lions," the Bike Derby results, "Lumo Marketing the Experience," and a section for children called "Kasi Mews" written by Kasi, a city kitty who comes to live in the bush. Aaron's editorial piece is titled "Transportation in Kenya," and mine, "Children Are Our Future."

On another recon day, we pick up a Maasai couple and their three children. When we drop them off in the market area, they say, *"Asholing,"* which means thank you in their language. The universe is on our side because on this trip we negotiate a rental agreement for a small house with potential just outside of Voi town.

The unfurnished home is made of cinder blocks painted teal. It has red concrete floors; jalousie windows with screens; a gray tile roof; a small covered porch at the front door; two small bedrooms, each with a window; a tiny kitchen with a countertop stove with two battered burners and room for a small fridge; an airy family room; and a separate attached bedroom for Jasmine, who will stay with us during the week. And yes, we have electricity and an indoor bathroom with a flush toilet and a slow drip shower with cold water. The nicely landscaped lot is entirely fenced, with a guard shed marking the front corner. All this for 15,000 ksh per month or $200.

I look forward to putting my design talents to the test with furniture handmade in Malindi, colorful fabrics from the Indian shops on Bishara Street in Nairobi, hand-woven baskets from Mombasa, and carpets from the Nakumat stores. We will also get a refrigerator for properly storing food, plus a bottled water dispenser. What a relief!

One evening we are invited to dinner with Hannah from Kasigau Ranch, and I'm grateful for the companionship of other women. She and her daughters are very friendly, and they want to know all about me, like how it is that I know how to drive a car. They can't believe I have children since I look so young and have such a good figure. *I love them!*

The next day we carry a father and his small daughter to Voi. She is around five years old and is so precious. She is heading to pick up her gift from her Canadian World Vision sponsor. World Vision is an international non-profit with focus on the well-being of all people, especially children. They run a child sponsorship program and operate on the theory that changing the lives of children facilitates overall growth and development in the community. I can't help looking back over the seat at her every so often. Her smile is infectious. When we arrive at the World Vision office, I lift her from the car. A light rain is falling. Her father is grateful, and the pride in his face for his daughter is heartwarming.

A trip to Mombasa in is the works so that we can take Kasi to Dr. Fazel's for a booster shot, and then we'll go to Malindi for furniture. We enjoy a relatively cool day, and

Kasi is so well-behaved; no more basket prison for her. After spending time with Dr. Fazel, we head up the coast to Malindi. We stop halfway there at a wonderful resort on Moonlight Bay. Aaron signs us in as writers, and we get an upgraded room. We should have been doing this all along. This becomes another one of my favorite places.

The next morning on the way to Malindi, Aaron is in an awful mood. Maybe it's because he can't find his meds. *Again!* When we first arrived in Kenya, he would let me read the letters he had written to his mother before he sent them and would also let me read her responses. I hadn't requested we follow this procedure, but lately I've noticed him writing her letters, addressing them, and quickly sealing them shut. Her responses are also closely guarded. I take note.

We both feel better after having lunch at the Old Man by the Sea restaurant, satisfying our hunger on delicious vegetarian lasagna. We are in Malindi, and I'm ready to explore. Malindi developed as part of the emerging Swahili civilization in the fifth through the tenth centuries. Portuguese explorer Vasco de Gama met with the Sheik of Malindi in 1498, and this precipitated the Portuguese Empire ruling Malindi from 1500 to 1630. We make a stop at The Pillar, a monument memorializing Vasco de Gama, built in 1498. The top of the limestone pillar bears a cross made of stone from de Gama's native Portugal.

As we drive on, I spot two cushioned wicker chairs, a wicker bed and mattress, and a "pouf" ottoman at a roadside shop. A hand-carved headboard is a true find.

I envision old and new friends alike congregating with us in the inviting environment we are creating for our new abode.

In memory of Maasai friends –
Moses and Kiyenni.

Meeting with Jane Goodall at Washington State University (WSU) to learn more about her Roots & Shoots youth action programs.

Presenting a wolf interpretive program as a park ranger at Albeni Falls Dam on Lake Pend Oreille in Idaho.

Trekking in the Himalayas with my son,
Douglas, and our Sherpa sidar, Anser Tsering.
Tsering climbed Everest in 1975 as a guide for
the first woman in history to reach
the summit.

A paradise home in the bush in Rukanga until a red spitting cobra enters.

The 35-kilometer road to Mt. Kasigau and the Banda in the village of Rukanga in Kenya. (Cobra Rock stands to the left in the foreground).

Looking into the eyes of the mountain gorillas, gentle giants, of Rwanda – a success story of protecting endangered species.

With Maasai Katoo and Kiyenni navigating our way to the Maasai wedding.

The Bride arriving to the Groom's manyatta from a neighboring boma.

Sharing wedding videos with the Maasai women during afternoon chi (tea).

Having fun with children who live with their families along the banks of the Omo River.

Young Hamar woman photographed at one of the market places along the Omo River. Her photo made the cover of NAI's magazine, Legacy, along with the featured story.

Young Maasai men celebrating at the wedding through chanting and demonstrating their incredible jumping skills.

National Association of Interpretation (NAI) Certified Guide Training (CIG) class for safari guides with Origins Safaris.

Initiates are solemnly waiting for the
Samburu Circumcision Ceremony to begin
in northern Kenya.

Herding cattle and goats along the banks of the Omo River in Ethiopia.

Some young men have taken up guns instead of spears as a way to protect their friends and families in the Omo River Basin.

Turning a House into a Home

One cannot divine nor forecast the conditions that will make happiness; one only stumbles upon them by chance, in a lucky hour, at the world's end somewhere, and holds fast to the days.

—Willa Cather

January 2004
Voi, Kenya

Aaron and I are moving to Voi today. I'm ecstatic! We pack what we can from the banda, load Kasi, and we are off on a new adventure. The downside of all this is leaving behind our Taita friends in the tiny village of Rukanga at the foot of Mount Kasigau. Saying goodbye to Hateb, Williamson, and Tempest brings tears to my eyes.

Arrival in Voi is nothing unusual for us, but this time we continue past the Tsavo Park Hotel and the football fields and climb a steep grade. We make a sharp right turn and then a quick left into the driveway of our new place.

It needs lots of work. We scrub the floors, wipe down the walls, and clean the glass windows. We discover we can walk out the back door and be at the Free World Club. This is where we have our first lunch. I challenge Aaron to a game of eight ball while we wait for our chicken sandwiches. During an afternoon break, we ride to the Voi Gate at Tsavo East National Park. Already, we see several impalas, a few dick-dicks, and several birds. We hope to get resident passes into the parks since tourist fees are extremely high.

Our first home project is to create a writing area on one wall using sawhorses and planks. We add two plastic chairs that we find down the hill at the market. We have learned that when living at subsistence levels as we did in the bush, one cannot enjoy the luxury of innovation; one must devote his or her time and energy to basic survival. This played out all around us in Rukanga.

Much of my time here will be spent writing and editing the *Kasigau Conservationist* newsletters, documenting our journey for those back home, and joining the team working closely with the Lumo Community Wildlife Sanctuary, three ranches that merged to form a conservancy back in 1997. The sanctuary is planning to have a grand opening supporting tourism in a few months, and we will be covering the event.

As we organize our desks, Kasigau believes we have assembled a playground for her. She pushes the pens onto the concrete floor, naps on the computer keyboard, and vaults from the desk into the jalousie windowpanes to get a better view of the insect population outside. Already Aaron and I are happy here. But happiness can be fleeting.

The Distar Restaurant is where we have our first dinner on our first night as residents of Voi. I have the Kenyan version of a cheeseburger, which is mainly a toasted cheese sandwich. Aaron has an egg sandwich minus the egg and he complains. One hour later a new sandwich is brought to our table, and now there are a couple of eggs in between the layers of bread. Aaron is happy for now, but later in the night, he awakens dog sick. He throws up uncontrollably, suffers severe abdominal pain, has clammy skin, and feels dizzy. *Will this trigger an epileptic seizure?* He has told me how dangerous a seizure can be for him. I do have a syringe of valium to inject if a seizure lasts longer than two minutes. I am beside myself; his life is in my hands.

In desperation at 3:00 a.m. I say, "Let's find the hospital."

In Voi, I only know places where we can get a cold drink, check email, and purchase groceries. Then I remember seeing a sign for a hospital from the front window of the Distar Restaurant earlier in the evening.

Upon arrival I see that the sign actually reads HOSPITAL/CLINIC/GERIATRIC & MATERNITY WARDS. We go in anyway and must climb up two flights of stairs. I feel sorry for Aaron and try to help him. The nurses find a bed among the row of metal cots housing thin mattresses with stained sheets. I can't bear this. Meanwhile Aaron is getting no relief. I finally back off and wait in the lobby. He is admitted.

Then even in my stressed state, I gain some comic relief. Has Aaron been admitted to the geriatric ward or the maternity ward? On relaying this story to my mother, a year later, she will ask the same question. I love my mother's sense of humor.

Meanwhile the nurses begin an IV drip with clean needles, I hope.

"He is an epileptic," I say. "He needs a doctor."

The doctor arrives thirty minutes later and does a blood test. "It is just a touch of malaria."

Is this the Kenyan explanation for every illness? Even in the bush villagers often complained about having malaria when it might just be an upset stomach or a headache.

The nurses offer me a cot next to Aaron. *Should I stay or should I go?* My emotions come and go on the wind that swirls around me here in Sub-Saharan Africa.

Even as a child, I never wanted to play doctor and certainly never considered a career in the health care field. So it is clear: I cannot stay in this place. I gently pat Aaron's shoulder to reassure him that I will be back in the morning. With a fair amount of guilt, I drive back to our house and through the gate, which I had inadvertently left open in my hurry to get him to the hospital. I catch myself looking anxiously in the rearview mirror. I do not get out to close the heavy wooden gate since I sense that someone has followed me. Maybe this wasn't such a good idea. I finally jump out of the car and run into the house. There are no locks on the doors so I prop a plastic chair under the doorknob of the front door and run into the bedroom.

I peek out the window. A car comes by, turns around, comes back, and pulls into the driveway. The lights and the engine go off. I watch for fifteen minutes and nothing happens, so I collapse in my sleeping bag on the floor. I wait in the still dark night and listen for the back door to open. Instead, I hear muffled voices outside my bedroom window. I lie still and eventually they fade into the night.

I stay in my sleeping bag and hold onto Kasi until first light. I love this cat, and she appears to love me. As my day begins, I creep out of the bedroom, make a cup of coffee, and walk out into the driveway, where I find empty beer bottles.

I walk down to the hospital to check on Aaron. He looks better but is still nauseated. He wants to come home, but he is still hooked up to the IV. I tell him about my scary night. The doctor arrives and says that Aaron will need to stay another twenty-four hours.

A young girl is waiting for me at the house gate when I return. Her name is Sora, and she says she wants to be my "house girl." I'm thrilled. I hire her temporarily, and her first day of work is very difficult. She helps me clean up the mess. The bedroom and bath are a disaster. I clean up the worst.

In the late afternoon as I'm walking back to the clinic, I hear Aaron yelling, "Are you okay?" I'm shocked to see Aaron and a nurse walking up the dirt road. She is holding the IV bag and tubing that is still attached to Aaron's wrist. With them is Maasai Kiyenni, the official greeter at the Tsavo Park Hotel.

Aaron explains, "I have hired this Maasai to watch over you tonight."

I hug Aaron and drive them all back to town and plan my evening. Tonight, Kasi and I will have a girl's slumber party. I write in my journal, and she plays a game of hiding in her basket and attacking my pen when I least expect it.

Just before sunset, Kiyenni comes to the back gate. We exchange "Jambo" since Kiyenni does not speak English and I only speak a little Swahili. Most Maasai have scars on their bodies, and I can't help but notice his. I point to the scars on his shoulder, and he pantomimes a delightful theatrical tale of when he was attacked by a lion, Simba, and how he fought it off with his club and killed it with his knife, *panga.* He shows me the teeth marks on his left shoulder and claw marks on his right hand. I grimace because I know that this must have been painful. His pure white teeth sparkle in the fading sunlight, and his eyes glisten as they absorb my dramatic reaction to his story. Already we have made a riveting connection that begins a unique relationship.

I invite Kiyenni to relax on the porch, where earlier today I placed a white plastic table with chairs. I provide hot tea and biscuits to his delight. I'm not sure how to behave, but having this tough warrior, who fought and killed a lion and survived, out on my porch tonight makes me feel so secure, I fall into the most glorious sleep.

I only awaken when I hear a strange sound, like someone pounding on metal pipes. Later I find out our water is turned off every night at ten and turned back on every morning at six. Air in the pipes causes this banging sound.

This will be my alarm clock for the next five months of small-town living in Kenya.

I peek out the window to see if my Maasai guard is still on the porch, but he's gone. Kasi and I play hide and seek while I make coffee. I believe she understands the game. She hides, and when I find her in another room, she jumps out and attacks me. We have a home.

The Maasai Connection

Everybody born comes from the Creator,
trailing wisps of glory.

—Maya Angelou

January 2004
Voi, Kenya

Aaron is released today. We walk home and find three Maasai warriors on our doorstep. They are dressed similar to Kiyenni in bright red cloth knotted on their left shoulders and draped loosely over their oiled, muscular bodies. They greet us and stand at attention. Their beaded jewelry is so strikingly beautiful that I just stare back and delay giving them a proper greeting.

Millions of beads found their way into Africa in exchange for slaves, spices, and ivory. They passed through ancient trade routes of Arabia, Portugal, Venice, India, and China. Africans have long traded beads and worn them as adornment, stringing them into earrings, bracelets, necklaces, headdresses, and even stitching them into the fabric of their clothing. I become a fan of beaded jewelry and proudly forgo gold, silver, and diamonds.

After proper greetings and several attempts to communicate, one warrior runs off and returns with Maasai Zachariah. He speaks English and has been summoned as an interpreter. Zachariah tells us that he spent seven years at a tourist camp in Tsavo East National Park and learned to speak English so that he might interact with the tourists on a more personal level. His friends heard we were looking for security guards, *askaris*. We weren't really looking for guards, but some residents and shops alike employ security guards, often Maasai because of their warrior reputation. It takes him the longest time to make them understand we already have a night guard. But then Aaron decides, and I agree, that one of them can cover the daytime duties. They say they will be back at four to show us their ID cards and then we must choose one of them to fulfill the position. Aaron and I agree that if we can provide employment for those searching for work, we can learn and gain an understanding of an ancient indigenous culture that thrives today.

At four o'clock sharp the Maasai are back on our porch. Aaron comes up with the idea of a coin toss. I demonstrate and then hand the coin to one of the guys. He tosses it high into the air. It hits the ground and he begins "jumping." His long braids are waving in the air as his body rises and falls to a rhythm chanted by his friends. I look in amazement and confusion. Zachariah tells us they think we will be choosing the one who is the best dancer.

We laugh and say no.

The other two toss coins. One coin lying on the ground has the etching of ex-President Moi facing skyward; the other two are blank.

"It's decided," I say. "The president will be working for us."

Katoo promises to be at work tomorrow. I'm thrilled to know that Zachariah lives here in Voi. If I have any communication issues, I'll be able to call him for assistance. He will become my go-to man in more ways than one.

Dinner is at the Free World Club. It's a local nightly gathering spot with a disc jockey and dance floor. Every weekend on Friday and Saturday nights, the music will be playing loudly until daybreak with a distinctive monotonous African beat. Young people pulsate with sexual energy until morning. Supposedly, a minister lived here before us. Hard to imagine.

Later in the evening when we return home, we find a small Maasai communal gathering on our front porch. We learn that this is a common occurrence among the Maasai brotherhood. We provide them blankets so they can be comfortable for sleeping if so desired in the tiny shed in the front corner of the compound. I provide chai tea and we communicate mainly with hand gestures, body language, and a few Maa words that Maasai Kiyenni teaches me. I make sure to learn the basic words, like hello, thank you, please, and excuse me. A common trust begins.

When we move to the parts of the body, Kiyenni points to them and says the Swahili word, or Maa word, and I say the English word. When we arrive at the buttocks, much laughter erupts when I repeat the Maasai word *elullie*. Next, we move to foods and the names of animals and birds. Eventually, I ask to know the names of his relatives and ancestors.

A man in town tells us that Westerners trust the Maasai even though none of the other forty-one tribes in Kenya do. He adds that if anyone were to suggest that a Maasai rob a white person, the Maasai would adamantly refuse, except for one caveat. Apparently, if we have cattle, they might steal them since God has ordained the Maasai to be in charge of all the cattle on earth.

Zachariah visits often and shares the myths and mysteries of the Maasai based on their oral history. Of all East Africa's ethnic groups, none is better known than the Maasai. Fiercely proud and traditional people, these semi-nomadic pastoralists made their first forays into East Africa during the fifteenth century. They were known as fearsome warriors, and as they moved down the Nile River, coming south in search of cattle-grazing land, they forced many other tribes out of the way.

I remark that I have seen Maasai driving cattle through Nairobi on the sidewalks. Zachariah tells me that Nairobi was Maasai land when the British arrived, and the Maasai still consider it their own. "Most of us don't like to live there because it's too cold," he adds. *"Baridi."*

Zachariah continues, "The two things valued most by us above all else are children and cattles. The cattles belong to the men. Women own the milk. Our common greeting is *'Keserian ingers? Keserian ingishu?'* How are the children? How are the cattles?"

The Maasai belief system and life itself is based on the ownership of cattle. These beasts are more than just a food source; they represent wealth and status. The Maasai regard any wild animal as unequivocally inferior to domestic livestock and particularly to cattle. So strong is this belief that the killing of any domestic animal by a wild beast is taken as a bad omen. If you eat the meat of this cow, you may be taking on the negative spirits within the dead animal. Because of these customs, wildlife has been spared wherever the Maasai have their traditional lands, notably in the Maasai Mara and Serengeti and the surrounding areas. There is one exception. All Maasai see lions as a symbol of strength, so every warrior must spear a lion before becoming a junior elder.

Today, a Maasai hunting a lion in a national park can be shot on sight, since all hunting has been banned in Kenya for over half a century.

Blessing the Rains

*Those who were dancing were thought to be insane by
those who could not hear the music.*

—Anonymous

January 2004
Voi, Kenya

E veryone in this part of Kenya has been saying for months now, "The rains are coming." The maize crop has failed, and the local villagers no longer trudge at daybreak with hoe in hand to their shambas or gardens. They sit listlessly on three-legged wooden stools outside the small shops on the village street - waiting, waiting. Some keep repeating, "God will provide," as their cattle and goats surrender to the drought.

Our cinder block house provides some relief from the heat. The jalousie windows allow us to control the direction of the air intake if and when there is any. We have purchased a fan for the bedroom to move the warm, stale air around. It's still too hot for sleeping. The traces of water in the river near our new home are green, thick, and virtually stagnant, barely moving. Time is also trickling by.

Then at 5:00 a.m. January 16, I awake to a strange new sound: a blessed breeze. The leaves on the acacia trees sing, and then rain begins to dance on the tile roof. I listen, remembering the heat lightning I watched late last night from the front porch with Maasai Kiyenni as it lit up Lion Hill. At that time, we were encouraging a storm to proceed to our area by waving it on saying, "Karibuni, welcome!"

I swear I can taste the moisture in the air, and so before daybreak, I shake Aaron. "Wake up, wake up. Let's go outside and bathe in the rain." Aaron, with sleep still in his eyes, yawns. I push him out of bed. "Hurry, it's still dark. No one will see us."

We sprint out the front door and dance naked to the music of the rain. I wash my hair and watch the suds stream down my body and then pool on the rich, brown dirt around my feet while I continue to move to the rhythm. Body and soul are baptized as one. Reborn, we run back into the house singing "Africa" by Toto, spring into bed, laugh, snuggle, and give thanks to the Rain God.

But the rain begins to fall in earnest so be careful what you wish for. Blowing rain hammers at the windows at daybreak, and it sounds like a river is flowing through our compound. A deluge is upon us. It rains and rains and rains. The wind picks up speed and howls like a hurricane barreling through our small space on this planet.

The violent showers continue to increase throughout the day and into the evening. Water pours from the eaves and gushes into the doorways. A fretful wind lashes at the windows. Clouds tumble over the horizon. The river over-flows its banks, and muddy water pours across our land-scape. It is the worst rain and thunderstorm I have ever witnessed. We are trapped in our house all day. Our Maasai friends, likewise, are trapped in theirs. All we can do is wave at them occasionally just to make sure they are okay.

Hot weather with no rain for months on end can be maddening; the sun burns the land but the sudden, over-whelming barrage of water and its resulting destruction can be just as maddening. The torrent continues into the night. When we finally make it into town the next day, we are told that no one has ever witnessed rain like this. Hous-es have been swept away, roads closed, and cattle are miss-ing. I'm learning about the changing tides on the continent of Africa. The rains are here.

Conflicting Air Currents

Give wherever the mind feels confidence.

—Shakyamuni Buddha

February 2004
Voi, Kenya

I'm feeling energized, and since Jasmine is late arriving, I mop and clean the floors with disinfectant and wash clothes with soap and the hot water that I've boiled on the stove. I'm actually having fun.

When I get ready to head to town, Alexandra drives up with Jasmine. The new seat belt law is still keeping matatus off the road. I remember Alexandra from Rob's place after the snake encounter and my muscles tense again. The day I met her, she was suffering from a hangover and was quiet, but today she is outspoken about her disgust for the matatu strike and just life in general. *Why does she trigger such a negative reaction in my gut?*

Jasmine and I walk to town, and buy new outfits for the trip to Mombasa. Aaron and I have agreed that we would like to take her to see her family. She is so happy and grateful.

The fabric we choose is a leafy pattern in beautiful shades of green. We also pick out new sandals. I think it is important for her to look good when she sees her ex-husband and their three children who live with him. She hasn't seen them in over three years. On our way home, Jasmine and I walk by the Voi Prison, which is just a small two-story structure. Normally guards patrol the gates, but today we don't see any. When we stop at the kiosk across from the gate to buy some charcoal for cooking, we hear a gunshot and then loud voices coming from inside. The streets are business as usual, and no one pays any attention to the ruckus. I'm concerned, but we continue on like the rest.

Jasmine wants me to meet her son and his family. We walk uphill for two miles to their village. The path to his house is lined with bags of bones. Jasmine tells me that her son collects these and that a man from Nairobi comes out and buys them. I think maybe he is a paleontologist hoping for a significant find.

Tonight, I'm writing stories to send back to the Northwest. They will be published in the Seattle District's *Flagship*, the Albeni Falls project newsletter *River Rumors*, and the local newspaper from Priest River, Idaho the *River Journal.* I play my favorite Neil Diamond CD, and Aaron and I both jump up and start singing and dancing. Sometimes we have so much fun together. The evening brings a heat lightning show followed by a full moon.

When I walk outside to get a better look, Kiyenni joins me, points to the moon, and says, "Alapa."

I repeat the Maa word and then point and say, "Moon."

He does his best to repeat the English word.

Because of the mosquitoes, I go back in the house and pack for the trip to Mombasa.

*

J asmine will be reunited with her family today. We make an early departure from Voi. I drive the first leg of the journey. When we stop to change drivers, Jasmine and I run to the bush for a bathroom break. Aaron drives through the rough part, and we cross on the Likoni Ferry to the south coast of Diani.

Saturday is a big market day, with pushcarts everywhere loaded to the hilt with every kind of product imaginable: vegetables, bunches of bananas, sugar cane, and building supplies. Of all the people here, people with pushcarts are the ones I worry the most about on the highway. They must balance their load while making their way down to the ferry. Then they must climb back up to street level once the ferry reaches Diani, an undertaking requiring major body strength. Aaron gets a feel for the process by getting out of the car and helping a man who is struggling with his cart of wooden poles.

I'm surprised when Jasmine knows exactly how to get to her ex's house. But then she tells me we're going to the home they shared. When they split, she went back to live with her parents in the village.

Jasmine is beaming wearing her new duds. We all walk up to the house, and the reunion with her three kids is touching. We leave immediately to allow them space.

Aaron and I look for a cottage for the night. We find one back at Moonlight Bay that suits our budget. Actually, it might be a perfect place to spend our last four months. All our furniture would fit here. The beach is secluded. Today the ocean is rough since we are getting the backlash of a hurricane in Mozambique or Madagascar. We swim anyway and then have a candlelight dinner overlooking the bay with the full moon reflecting on the water while one of my favorite songs by Foreigner, "I Want to Know What Love Is", plays on a loud speaker. Two other couples are at the outdoor restaurant. Guards stand by with bows and arrows.

Our bedroom is large, with a four-poster bed and tons of mosquito netting that envelops us during our passionate lovemaking. We end up wrestling our way out of its grip and laugh so much that it takes us forever to get to sleep. We get up early to head to Mombasa town. Our first stop is for coffee and strudel at the Book One store. Our plan is to find fabric for *shukas* for our Maasai guards. We land in a shop with lots of Maasai fabrics. A rather large Maasai mama is buying beads. When we ask to see fabrics, she grabs my hands. She points to just the right patterns for our guys. Then the bargaining begins: 3,000 is the starting price, but she negotiates down to 2,600. I believe Maasai

Mama has enjoyed all the interaction more than anyone else.

At the cottage, a fisherman is waiting for us with a red snapper. We graciously pay for the fish, and the chef at the bar prepares it for us. It is blackened and fried with baked potatoes and veggies on the side. It's one of the best meals we've had in Kenya.

"We cannot eat all this wonderful meal, so please share it with your staff," I offer.

They are delighted and join us in the dining room.

In the afternoon I suggest we drive to Shimba Hills, the home of the sable antelope.

It's twenty-five kilometers up to a rainforest, and the car has trouble climbing the hill. I show my passport and visa at the gate. But we have a problem: Aaron does not have his passport or visa with him. The gatekeeper says, "No passport, no entry."

Aaron jumps out of the car and says, "I'll stay behind. Let my wife enter." The young guard is thrown off balance by this action and now decides we can both enter for a short period of time.

The Shimba Hills Lodge is made of logs and features 120 meters of wooden walkways. On a bridge out into the trees, we catch a glimpse of a fish eagle and some large hornbills. Inside, we are treated as guests and are given drinks. I realize we are crashing a party, and when I take the drink, I giggle, remembering how my son Derek and I accidently crashed a $200-a-plate boat reception on the

Tennessee River a few years back. We had just left a Native American exhibit and lecture in Russell Cave and were still up for some more entertainment. When we saw bright lights on a boat on the river, and we walked on board to find out what was happening. A greeter escorted us into a ball room and invited to indulge in the wine and food bar. When patrons began to engage us in conversation and ask questions, we realized it was time to jump ship. When we were almost safely out of the throngs of people, the boat captain approached and wanted to know why we were leaving so early. I made up some story and thanked him for putting on such an impressive event even though we still had no idea what event we had crashed. Back on land, Derek and I ran back to our car doubled over in spontaneous laughter. A few days later I found out the event was to honor the donors who supported a band of international students who were traveling and performing at stops along the river.

Here at Shimba Hills, Aaron and I laugh as we sneak off to a secluded corner and revel in the view over the pond as we meander out to the boardwalk. We do not see the sable antelope but appreciate the excursion and the fun, anyway.

The next day we head back to Mombasa, pick up Jasmine and depart by way of the ferry, where we provide a young French couple a ride to Mombasa. They climb in the back, and we drop them off at the bus/matatus station. A stop at Dr. Fazil's to pick up Kasi leads to an invite for breakfast, once again a welcome treat. Kasi sleeps on Jasmine's lap all the way back to Maungu.

By the time we get home it's 6:00 p.m. Kasi is so happy to be back home that she runs down the hallway and slides on all fours.

On Valentine's Day we meet Malachite and Weldon at Free World for dinner. We have the specialty chicken, good conversation, and we dance. A guy keeps trying to dance with me, and Aaron keeps pushing him away. When I go back to my seat, I see snakelike Alexandra walk in. *That's it! Her tattoos trigger my muscle memory of the red-spitting cobra. So sorry, Alexandra.*

Malachite immediately pulls her onto the dance floor. He kisses her on both cheeks and then on the lips. He looks over at me. I stare back at him. A part of me feels jealous. Aaron and I leave at 10 p.m. I awake the next day wondering if Alexandra ended up in Malachite's bed, the one he showed me at his office where he sleeps some nights when he works late.

*

T oday we take a trip to TDC to meet with Leigh about offering a CIG course for his safari guides. In the past, he would have comped our lunch, but today we are charged twenty dollars per person. I'm shocked and realize he may have hard feelings about our leaving Rukanga. I assumed all was well.

Before leaving TDC, we see a vehicle that was mauled by an elephant. Koral, a TDC safari guide, was driving and had two French women with him. The elephant charged and used its large tusks to lift the vehicle by the front end and throw it against a tree. Then it used its trunk to roll the vehicle over a couple of times. There are holes in the canvas top where the tusks came through. Amazingly, no one was seriously injured. They lost radio contact and began walking back, but another guide came along and rescued them. Of course, both women flew back to France the next day, saying they had seen enough of Africa.

*

Having a car has given us so much freedom to come and go pretty much as we please, and today we drive through the grasslands near Nairobi in search of cool breezes. The road from Voi to Nairobi is the dividing line between Tsavo East and Tsavo West National Parks. Along one section of the drive, a particularly beautiful rock formation stands in the distance to the west.

"I'm visualizing a kudu coming down from behind that rock," I say.

Less than five minutes later, a male lesser kudu antelope emerges from the vegetation and crosses the road in front of us. The kudu proceeds very slowly as if to make sure we get a good look at the white stripe down his back and the twelve white stripes branching down his sides. A close-up of the spectacular spiral horns reminds me of the erratic sound that bellows out when locals blow through these horns turned into musical instruments.

A small herd of zebras and many birds: eagles, falcons, and colorful bee-eaters, parade themselves in front of us. After we leave the national park area, the road deteriorates rapidly. Progress from here is very slow.

We arrive at the Zebra Lodge, a well-kept secret where Aaron and I spend most of our time in Nairobi. The place is a perpetual blessing where we are able to decompress and relax while preparing for our meeting with Steve Turner in the morning.

*

We get lucky and find a parking space right in front of Fedha Towers where Steve's office is located. He is hospitable and understands why we had to move out of the bush. After we left Rukanga, a villager was bitten by a poisonous snake in the middle of the night and was lucky to survive. We end up chatting for over an hour about scheduling NAI's CIG four-day workshop for his safari guides. This will be a tremendous amount of work for me but also a feather in my cap to be the first NAI member to facilitate this specialized training on an international level.

I'm proud and won't charge for my services; therefore, Steve has volunteered to pay for our hotel stays during the three workshops that we schedule.

Back in Voi, I find an African surprise. When I enter the shower room to rinse off, I find it swarming with insects that look like giant mosquitoes. Kasi goes crazy jumping around after them. There are hundreds, and the screen is full with more banging to get in. When I open the toilet room, it is also full. I turn back into the hallway and switch on the overhead light. The bugs start flooding into that space and circle. Aaron is in bed. I run and jump in with him. He finally gets up, puts on rain gear, and sprays Raid like wild. I grab Kasi, and we burrow under the covers. The bugs, better known as *du-dus* here, leave the house by whatever means they came in. It was like being in an Alfred Hitchcock movie.

Vision Scare

*My best hope is every bit as likely to occur as
my worst fear, so I have no reason to give more
weight to my negative assumptions.*

—Courage to Change

March 2004
Mombasa, Kenya

I get up like a whirlwind but slow to a snail's pace when white flashes start going off in my left eye. I'm afraid something is seriously wrong. It's raining gently and I feel like it is a clue that I need to be gentle with my mind, body and spirit today. I spend most of the day in bed with my eyes closed. When these flashes haven't subsided by late afternoon, I call Dr. Hanif. He and his wife, Kat, the owner of Ashtech, meet me in town. We have become friends and have shared meals together recently. He sees a ripple on the surface of my eye.

"You need to get to the Eye Clinic in Mombasa ASAP to see the retina specialist, Dr. Helena," he says.

I call Dr. Helena, and she can see me tomorrow. My day-time symptoms are improving somewhat but what a light show I experience tonight. *I'm scared.*

*

We leave at 5:00 a.m. Our two Maasai guards ask to join us. Kiyenni is finally getting his trip to Mombasa. I sit in the back seat and try to baby my eye by avoiding looking directly into the rising sun. I'm apprehensive about the drive. I ask Aaron to be extra careful.

Halfway to the coast, we come upon tree branches lining the roadway. They take the place of orange cones to warn other travelers of an accident ahead. We proceed slowly and come upon an overturned semi with broken glass spread all over the highway. The smell of beer permeates the air. A Tusker truck carrying the Kenyan beer of choice is lying on its side practically in the middle of the road. Four or five other trucks are pulled off to the side. We're not sure if they're involved in the accident or if they've stopped to help a fellow driver. People are running down from the hills to the right, and I think they must be good Samaritans. As the scene unfolds, I'm horrified at what I'm witnessing. Villagers swarming around the truck carting off crates of beer; some are running back up the hill with cases of beer balanced on their heads. More arrive from the meadows on the left and do the same. This is concerning but we proceed along the glass-strewn highway jockeying around the Tusker truck so we won't be late for my appointment. A stop at the police checkpoint a few miles down the road gives us a chance to regroup and report the accident.

As we approach Mombasa and cross the harbor, the guys show visible signs of being frightened. I don't understand why they're so fearful. Do they see a boat and think it might be the ferry? Kiyenni looks at me and points to the circular marks on his cheeks where he was branded as a baby and says, "Maasai, no ferry." I assure them we will not take them on the ferry. As we approach town, I watch more of their reactions. They are most interested in the cattle they see. This is no surprise. They do not even give the women walking along the road a second glance.

We find the Lighthouse Eye Clinic by 8:30 a.m. Dr. Helena is very busy because it's Children's Day. Aaron and the guys wait in the parking lot. Once I'm in the reception area, I sit on a wooden chair across from a family with a young child. I believe they are Muslims. She is petite and attractive in her black veil dress with black lace—married, I suspect, since she does show her face but not her hair. The father, a little on the pudgy side but definitely the master of his family, is dressed rather casually in black shorts, a T-shirt, and sandals. The grandfather, who hovers over the setting, cements the patriarchal family structure. The child is a boy of six or seven and has a patch over one eye. A clinic assistant comes out and removes the patch. The boy cries out for his mother to protect him, much like my son Douglas cried out to me when his broken arm was being set in the emergency room, and how my son Derek cried out before being taken into surgery. A mother can only stand by, feeling helpless to protect her young in a situation like this. This child has a large cut under the eye, and the eyelid is bruised and swollen. I want to ask what happened to him, but I know it is not for me to interfere. All I can do is feel empathy for this baby who's in obvious pain. As they wait to see the doctor, the mother tries her best to comfort her son, while the patriarchal twosome stands by at a distance.

This child has a large cut under the eye, and the eyelid is bruised and swollen. I want to ask what happened to him, but I know it's not for me to interfere. All I can do is feel empathy for this baby who's in obvious pain. As they wait to see the doctor, the mother tries her best to comfort her son, while the patriarchal twosome stands by at a distance.

When they are called into the examining room, the two male figures take the child and tell the mother to stay outside in the waiting room. By the look on her face, I can see this causes her much anguish. I become aligned with her and feel like I've left my body to share her pain. We are across the room from one another, but occasionally make eye contact. She cries, and I cry.

When we hear a muffled sound coming from the examining room, she gets up and stands at the door. She closes her eyes and appears to be praying. I'm called for eye drops and miss the reunion of mother and son, but when I see the doctor, I inquire of the boy's condition.

He says, "Not good."

It takes me some time to separate myself from their predicament. I walk outside and talk to Aaron about the situation, and this helps. As my eyes blur from the drops, so does my connection to the family. Now I'm immersed in my own dilemma. *Will I lose my eyesight? Will I have to have surgery? Will my eye heal?*

Two hours later, when I come out with my pupils still dilated, Aaron wants to know what the doctor said. Apparently, my retina looks okay but I need to be vigilant and return within twenty-four to forty-eight hours if anything changes. The flashes can be a normal occurrence as the eye ages. I'm so relieved.

Now we are ready to head to the ocean and have some fun. We stop at the beach by Lynn and Paul's place and walk down a sandy path flanked by two walls of stone with bougainvillea splashing a torrent of color over them. I feel like we are walking through a rainbow. At the end is this beautiful site, the aquamarine ocean. I'm so elated that I rush to the water with Maasai Kiyenni and Moses on either side. We enter the surf with our sandals still on. I wonder if they're amazed at how warm the water is. I beckon them out farther, and they make it to thigh depth. Aaron photographs us. I begin to float, and they laugh when they see my feet and sandals above the surface.

Kiyenni picks up a handful of water and puts it to his mouth. "Drink, drink?"

"No, no," I say.

Next, he wants to know if there is a monster fish nearby. Maybe he has heard about Jonah and the whale. Moses strips down to his shorts and even gets rid of his knife. He comes back into the water and plays as if he is swimming.

We walk down the beach as far as the rock outcropping. I find a large flat sand area and spell out each of their names, proof that Kiyenni and Moses have seen the ocean. Their smiles convey that they're grateful. I am grateful that I will not lose my eyesight.

We Are Family

Love is patient and kind.
Love is not jealous or boastful, it is
not arrogant or rude, love does not
insist on its own way.

—1 Corinthians 13:4-7

March 2004
Voi, Kenya

Tonight, I show Kiyenni and Moses our digital photos from the ocean and they laugh hysterically. I make phone calls for them while they teach Aaron how to do animal calls, the vocalizations of the hyena sounds like a human giggling. Now I'm hysterical.

Moses tells the story of how his grandmother slayed a lion that came into the Manyatta when all the men and warriors were gone stealing cattle. She is famous throughout the Maasai reservation. Once again Kiyenni shows his Simba scars and Moses points to his self-inflicted scars; some by burning, others by a knife. I stay up late and play cards with the guys just so I can watch them pantomime more of their interesting stories.

In the morning we get an early start to Nairobi. My oldest son, Douglas, and his girlfriend, Melissa, should be on their way after their layover in London. We stop at Hunter's Lodge, one of our favorite lunch spots on the way. Before I know it, I'm standing at the Nairobi International Airport arrival gate waiting for my son. Tears well up in my eyes. Aaron and I watch for two hours for my firstborn to appear, but he never does. We try to check the passenger manifest, but no go. We leave the airport not knowing for sure what happened, but I suspect we have the wrong day. For sure he'll be here tomorrow. We check in at the Fairview Hotel and spend the rest of the day relaxing.

The next day we arrive at the airport awaiting the same daily flight from London, and there they are coming down the stairs from baggage claim. *Hooray!* After lunch at the hotel, we employ a driver to take the four of us on a tour of Nairobi. They are so excited to practice speaking Swahili with our young driver. We hit one of my favorite places, the Animal Orphanage in Nairobi National Park, and are given permission to join two young cheetahs in their caged area. They play with us like small kittens. It's a delightful interaction. Doug and Melissa want to know if we've been given special consideration because we are white, educated, and have money and connections.

"Yes," I say, "fortunately or unfortunately, all the above."

I'm able to leave a handsome tip since Douglas brought my bank debit card, my American Express credit card, and

$500 in cash from home. It's such a relief to be my own person again.

When we travel with Doug and Melissa back to Voi, they find out all about the contrasting Kenyan road system. We come through the national park, and they get to see their first African wildlife, baboons and zebra. Melissa has a new camera and enjoys filming. They're excited to be in Africa, and I'm excited to have them here. They both love our little home and Kasigau. They were prepared for the bush originally, so they are pleasantly surprised at our comfortable abode.

Today we walk the streets of Voi, and I introduce them to some of our friends. We meet Heather for lunch, and we all enjoy hearing about her crazy escapades as the local Peace Corps worker. She has a great sense of humor. After dinner we show Douglas and Melissa our photos on the laptop. We're sorry they won't get a chance to meet Katoo and Kiyenni, who are headed home to their villages.

Tonight Aaron, Melissa, and I are in the kitchen trying to do dishes and reorganize the cupboard shelves. I suggest a more organized way to proceed.

Aaron yells, "Why don't you just bug off!"

Not wanting any confrontation, I say, "I'll finish this in the morning."

I'm humiliated to have my son and his girlfriend see me treated with such disrespect. I stayed in my marriage longer than I should've because I didn't want to put my children through a family breakup and subject them to

204 · *A Whirlwind Year in Africa*   *Part II*

the pain I felt as a child. But in the end, I had to make a choice to protect them and myself from an escalating situation in hopes that one day they would understand and respect me for doing so.

Aaron is generally fun and loving when we are alone but has a tendency to change his tone when we are with others especially my family and friends. I express frustration when Aaron displays this rude behavior, and my reaction, as opposed to a non-reaction, I believe, is good. He apologizes, something he's good at. We go to bed a bit unsettled, wake early, talk it through, and then make love. This has become our established pattern of behavior, which may not be a good thing.

The next day we decide to head out to Rukanga, TDC, and Rukinga Ranch. Douglas and Melissa are amazed at the beauty of the area. Aaron and I haven't visited in six weeks, and we feel like we are seeing it again for the first time through their eyes. When we reach Kent's shop in Rukanga, word begins to spread, and before we know it, Tempest arrives. It's an emotional meeting. We hug and hold hands for a long time. Hateb shows up next, and he and Aaron have a similar reunion. Heather comes on her bicycle and proceeds with us. We head up to the banda and all the kids are shaking hands with Melissa and Douglas. Now we meet Williamson and have another warm welcome. We are family again and congregate outside on the wooden furniture under a shade tree at the foot of Mt. Kasigau. Photos are taken and then it's time to leave.

Everyone has enjoyed meeting my firstborn and his *Rafiki* (friend).

We stop by one of my favorite shops in the village. I want my son to meet Grace. When Grace sees me, she starts crying. We hug. She tells me that her husband, Matay, has been killed in an auto accident on the Nairobi-Mombasa Highway. Sadness envelops me. It's hard to move on.

Back in Voi, Jasmine makes chapattis, beans, and samosas for dinner. Doug and Melissa love them. Kasi enjoys playing and teasing our guests and vice versa. We plan to drive through Tsavo East tomorrow on the way to Malindi, a new route for us. We have been told that it will be dangerous because of *shiftas*: Somalis, who may try to rob us. So we invite Moses to accompany us. He's elated.

Aaron and I luck out and get into Tsavo East National Park for the resident rate. We detour to Laguna Falls and approach the edge of the gorge. Peering fifty or sixty feet down, we see the whitewater rushing through a space that is only twelve feet wide. The sides of the chasm are a sculpture of fins, bowls, and bulges, all polished by the water. We walk along a quarter mile of narrows and have to shout above the roar to say anything to one another. I wonder if everyone is thinking the same thing I am: *If I slip and fall, I'm dead and gone.*

We detour to Galdessa Camp to see Moses's brother. The camp is like an oasis in the desert. It belongs in

Architectural Digest. I can't get enough of this beautiful place. I ask Melissa to take lots of photos. I'm glad we made the detour to both places.

We follow the river to the coast. Our bottled water is almost boiling, and we long for a cold drink. We stop at Buffalo Camp and get a warm soda – it's better than our water.

Melissa says, "Ice, please."

Our server laughs. "This is the savannah."

I think about how Heather and I miss ice so much and how we have both stopped asking.

What Aaron and I ask for today is an escort, something the park rangers at the Tsavo gate advised.

The ranger in residence says, "Sorry, the rifle carrying escort rangers have already left for Malindi." We proceed since we have Maasai Moses with us. Aaron lets Douglas drive. I ride shotgun. The road is horrendous. Then Douglas lets Melissa take over for a while. We still have ninety-three kilometers to go when Aaron, who has been sleeping in the back, wakes up, sees Melissa, and yells, "Why are you swerving all over the road?"

Douglas yells back, "Aaron, calm down! Melissa has never driven this car, and she is just trying to help out."

Aaron decides he'll drive, and we fly down the road. Thank goodness the surface has improved.

As darkness descends, I take the wheel. We pass through small villages where many of the residents are huddling around fires. Candles glow in the shops. Many people walk or ride bicycles along the road trying to get home. We detour to Watamu and get cottages at Ocean Sports next to Hemmingway's Hotel for the night. We have a late dinner and then collapse in bed.

The next day is a beach day and what a glorious day it is, sunny and beautiful. We swim and take a glass-bottom boat ride out past the reef. Douglas, Melissa, and I have our first snorkeling experience. I refuse to use the breathing tube, so I guess it isn't really snorkeling for me. The fish are incredible, and I especially like the colorful parrotfish. On our way back to shore, we stop on a large sandbar and all get out and play. Aaron drags me along the length of the bar by one hand as I float on my back. The water is so clear. Moses frolics with us. He finds a starfish and picks it up. Melissa captures an incredible photo of him walking in the surf.

Aaron and I take a long stroll over to Turtle Bay, one of the places where sea turtles lay their eggs. We are careful not to step on the nests even though we walk back in complete darkness.

*

Our return to Voi is uneventful. We put Douglas and Melissa on the train back to Nairobi. We're all so tired that our goodbyes are rushed and inadequate. "*Karibuni tena*, you are welcome to come again."

Later I hear their train hit a giraffe in the wee hours of the morning, condition unknown, causing tardiness to Nairobi. They did catch their flight back to the U.S., but both suffered a gastric illness from food they shared with other passengers on the train.

I'm already missing them.

Resident Aliens

Patience is the key to paradise.

—A Turkish proverb

April 2004
Ngorongoro Crater, Tanzania

We've been in Kenya for over six months. Our visas are running out, and we must leave temporarily. I want to go to Rwanda to see the mountain gorillas. Our friend, Steve, says he can arrange this for us. Then Rob, our British acquaintance from Rukinga Ranch, makes a suggestion to Aaron: "Just cross the border into Tanzania, go to the Ngorongoro Crater, and return in a few days. *Hakuna matata.*"

Aaron bites. "It will be cheaper," he says. I'm willing to pay for our trip to Rwanda but he still says, "No."

So, instead of flying to Kigali, Rwanda, we prepare to drive to Tanzania taking Maasai Moses with us. On the way back, we will stop in Moses's village and pick up his wife, Nasha, and his baby daughter, Moresia. He has asked us to film their traditional dance.

He adds, "We will slaughter a goat to welcome you."

The road to Taveta is rough. It takes us three hours. Moses is excited to be on safari. But the border crossing is frustrating. Moses has the freedom to walk across the border at any time because he's a Maasai and because we're in the Maasai Reserve, which falls on both sides with half in Tanzania and half in Kenya. But he is not permitted this time since he's in a car with *mzungus* (white people).

A sinister-looking official adds, "He'll also need a passport."

I wait with the vehicle at a café while Aaron takes Moses for passport photos. Valerie, a local, joins me for a soda. When I try to pay, she says, "No, just for my friend."

Aaron and Moses return, and I'm jealous. Moses looks terrific even in his passport photos.

Eventually we're back on the road to Arusha, Tanzania. The landscape changes to green and lush. Women weave down the sides of the road wearing banana headdresses, colorful sarongs, and carrying babies on their backs. The roads are paved and smooth, not full of the potholes we've become accustomed to. The people are friendly. Maasai in their bright-red *shukas* wave to Moses as we pass.

On the rim of the crater we find an ideal resort. We get two cabins, or *manyattas* as they are called here. Some Africans seem to find it distressing that we provide our Maasai friends their own rooms, the same as ours, instead of letting them stay in the staff quarters. This is a decision we've made and for us it's the right decision, plus the guys enjoy acting like tourists in their own country. Before Moses retires to his room, we discuss the time that we'll meet for dinner. He points to his watch—little hand on the six, big hand on the twelve. I shake my head yes.

This meal turns out to be a time for amusement. Maasai Moses has his first experience with a buffet. I take him around and try to explain all the choices. Then I leave him on his own. He heads back to the table, and the manager runs alongside with such a comical, concerned, look on his face. Moses has taken a large chunk of cheese that was made to slice. I laugh. Aaron saves the day by calmly slicing the cheese into three sections and putting a large piece on each of our plates. The frustrated manager retreats.

In the morning as we prepare to go on our game drive, Aaron says, "You drive down into the crater." It is a steep descent and I have my foot on the brake most of the way. This huge caldera is the world's largest crater with a diameter of ten miles. It hosts thousands of large animals including some of Tanzania's last remaining black rhino. It's amazing to see so many species in one isolated area. There are buffalo, wildebeest, antelope, zebra, hippos, and a flock of grey crowned cranes, the national bird of Tanzania.

∗

A surprise awaits us as we return to the border to cross back into Kenya at the end of our little safari. The border boss claims there's a new policy. "You haven't left East Africa, which is now Uganda, Kenya, Tanzania, so we cannot permit reentry to Kenya." He smiles with enormous satisfaction at our misfortune. I'm livid, not with the border boss, but with Aaron for assuming this would be a slam dunk. Moses, obviously frustrated, walks across to go to his home village. I'm really disappointed since we were going to meet his wife and daughter. *Now what?*

We opt for a drive to the Kilimanjaro airport to catch a flight to Johannesburg, South Africa. In flight I imagine I can see the mountain gorillas waiting for me, and I can't stop my tears from flowing. Aaron looks away.

Johannesburg is a large modern city. We even find 'Pringles' at the local bar. Mainly we stay in our room and rest for the weekend. Tomorrow we fly back to Kilimanjaro via Dar es Salaam.

A cloudy day leaves us disappointed because Mount Kilimanjaro is not visible, not even from the air. We're surprised to find our car still parked at the airport and intact. Then another surprise awaits us at the Taveta border crossing. The border boss says, "Okay, you can enter Kenya." We are relieved. Then he demands U.S. dollars for our visas.

I say, "We have no U.S. dollars. Please, take Kenyan shillings."

"*Hapana*, you must go to the bank in town and exchange shillings for dollars."

I don't know where there's a bank, but I head out on foot. Of course, there's only one bank in town, and it's closed.

Upon return to the border, I find Aaron standing toe-to-toe with boss man arguing about some unrelated issue. *Heaven help me!*

I interrupt, "The bank is closed."

The boss grins as if he already knew this. "Then you'll have to wait until tomorrow."

In frustration, I speak my mind. "Then we will have to sleep here in your office."

Of course, this is the last place I want to be spending the night. It is dark, dank, and there are geckos climbing all over the walls. I can already feel them crawling on me. As night falls and we are still sitting in his office, he suddenly remembers that there might be U.S. dollars in the safe. And there they are. I suppose he knew it all along and was waiting for a bribe. He quickly exchanges our Kenyan shillings for dollars, and we are on our way home, finally, after a barrage of unplanned expenses. The positive aspect of this fiasco: we are now resident aliens.

The Long Rains

There was a roaring in the wind all night.
The rain came heavily and fell in floods.

—**William Wordsworth**

Shifting Trade Winds

Catch the trade winds in your sails.
Explore. Dream. Discover.

—Mark Twain

April 2004
Voi, Kenya

When my palm was read several years ago and it fore-told of a life of travel, I thought I'd already done the traveling. At that time, I had been to all forty-eight states in the continental U.S. as well as Canada and Mexico with my traveling sidekicks, my mother and baby sister. Now here I am on the other side of the world in a different life with new potential.

I'm orchestrating the first CIG workshop in Kenya. It's being held, practically in my backyard, at the Free World Club. USAID is sponsoring the event, bringing together the Kasigau Conservation Trust Banda managers, the Tai-ta-Taveta Wildlife Forum representatives, and the Lumo Sanctuary scouts. Twenty-five men and women guides will be participating in this program authorized by the NAI.

The purpose of the workshop is to train interpreters on how to connect visitors to the important natural, cultural, and historical resources at their parks, nature centers, historical sites, aquariums, zoos, and anywhere that people come to learn. Once that connection is made, the desire to preserve the resource will be established and promoted.

On our first day there is nervous energy illuminating the area as we congregate in the outdoor shelter to begin class. After the morning introductions, one of the most important parts, I share the goals and objectives of the workshop. Having taught the course several times when preparing summer rangers in developing new and exciting programs for family campers, I'm fairly familiar with the material. I want Aaron to be my assistant, but to be official he needs to take the course and pass. He is agreeable and joins in with the rest. Since I have created an expedited process for Aaron, I suggest that he do his oral presentation on the second day of class so that he can become certified as an instructor. This way, the new recruits will be able to see what is expected of them on the last day of the four-day class. Aaron has already bragged to me how experienced he is at public speaking, so I'm confident about his upcoming demonstration. He'll be showcasing his favorite animal, the giraffe, that stands tall and proud, just as he does.

After morning tea on the second day, Aaron is ready. I introduce him to the group as the assistant instructor. His presentation must last twenty to thirty minutes and cover most of the class materials using universals, analogies, tangibles and intangibles, and emotional connections. He also must make sure that everyone in his audience can relate to the material he presents. Aaron starts out strong, but within five minutes he has forgotten his speech. He stumbles and mumbles. I have to prompt him. The students look bewildered. He has a slideshow to enhance his performance but has trouble accessing it. I intervene and set it up. He finishes after only fifteen minutes. I spend the next hour inviting the students to point out the positives and negatives of Aaron's presentation so that this will be a sample of what to do and what not to do.

In the evening, Aaron and I can't stop laughing about the day's events. I even get kudos from him on my quick response and recovery in that awkward situation.

On April Fool's Day, Aaron and I are up early grading the open book tests the students had to complete on their first day. These tests make up half their grade; the other half is the oral presentation. We are both sitting at our homemade desk, each working on a set of tests, when Aaron begins clicking his teeth just like Kasi does in excitement when she sees a gecko on the wall. I think Aaron is playing an April fool's joke on me.

"Aaron, don't make fun of Kasi," I say.

He doesn't stop. I look over at him and realize that he's not playing around. He's having a seizure. My worst fear is coming true.

His whole body is shaking. I've never seen him or anyone else have a seizure. I quickly remember that I need to make sure he doesn't injure himself, so I get behind him and wrap my arms around his forearms and chest and hold him tightly to the chair. His body is rigid.

I repeat over and over, "I love you. I love you. I love you."

His body becomes limp after a few minutes, way too many minutes for me. I'm already thinking about running to the refrigerator to obtain the vial of valium that may or may not still be potent. It's hard to know how many minutes have gone by.

He slowly becomes alert and says, "I guess I had a seizure. Please help me get to the bedroom to lie down."

He's almost twice my size, so I struggle to assist him down the hall. He tells me that he must stay relaxed or another seizure may happen. My stress level is astronomical.

Class is about to begin, so I must leave him alone and do my best. I can barely concentrate on the day's activities, so I give the students lots of free time to plan and practice the oral presentations they will be delivering tomorrow. At lunch, I run home to check on Aaron. He's feeling better. In the afternoon he comes moseying over to the class and that freaks me out. He wants to help, but I ask him to please just sit and rest. We make it through day three.

On the fourth day, the students give their presentations. I must determine grades of pass or fail. This is so difficult since over half the class has already failed the written part of the open book exam. But to my surprise, almost everyone's oral presentation is extraordinary. *I guess Aaron's sample presentation helped after all.* Everyone passes. I am overwhelmed by their abundant appreciation.

On April 22, Earth Day, Aaron's birthday, I surprise him with a trip to the Voi Wildlife Lodge (VWL) and gift him a membership to the spa. *Actually, I gift it to both of us.* They have a wonderful open-air lap pool and workout facility overlooking a watering hole in Tsavo East National Park. Aaron resists at first, but after we do a serious workout, take a relaxing swim in the lap pool, and have a drink out at the Gazebo Bar, he is on board and thanks me. Lunch is pizza at the Silent Resort, the best. On the way home we stop at New Generations and pick up a chocolate cake mix and even find something called chocolate cake coating.

While Aaron naps, I help Jasmine write letters to her three children in Mombasa while baking my first layer cake in Kenya. I bake each layer separately in a skillet on the propane gas burner. I keep the gas on low for ten minutes, then turn it off and let the baking continue for another fifteen. Magnificent! Aaron smells the cake and comes out to the kitchen. He melts the chocolate coating in a double boiler to near perfection. We ice the cake and are ready to celebrate.

Our Kenya friends, including Maasai Zachariah, are all excited to see how we celebrate birthdays. The six of us sing, or really just the two of us, and after Aaron blows out the candles, he cuts the cake.

Kiyenni looks at the cake and asks, "Cow?"

I laugh.

Zachariah and Katoo ask, "Blood pudding?"

They consume it *pole, pole.* (very slowly).

"Do you like it?" I ask.

Kiyenni gives it a thumbs up.

I'm not convinced, so I call his bluff and offer him another piece. He's panicked and waves his arms, "*Hapana, hapana*," one of the first Swahili words he taught me.

Zachariah surprises me and gives Kiyenni a compliment. "Kiyenni is a good teacher."

There are times I sense tension between Kiyenni and Zachariah, but not tonight. Aaron believes that they are both vying for my attention or affection. I smile. Kiyenni picks up two of Kasi's bouncy balls. My inner child kicks in, and I set up the playing field. The long hallway with our orange washbasin at the end is perfect. I start the game by bouncing one of the balls down the hallway into the basin. Getting both balls in is ten points. Zachariah is reluctant to play but does so after much coaching from Aaron.

Once we begin, Kasi comes to investigate. After watching Aaron take his turn, she climbs in the basin and lies down.

"She has entered the game as the goalie," I say.

She bats at the balls as they reach the goal, sometimes stopping them from entering so we cannot score.

Kiyenni is petrified of reaching in the basin with Kasi to retrieve the balls, so Katoo has to get them for him by holding Kasi by the scruff of the neck or diverting her attention with hand movements. I find it interesting that most of the Maasai I have met seem to be afraid of domestic cats.

When birthday boy gets *choka sana* (very tired), we say our goodbyes, "*Ole seri.*"

I hear the guys outside laughing late into the night.

The next day I want to continue the birthday celebration so we to go the VWL for dinner. By the time we get there I'm so hungry that my stomach is starting to cramp and spasm. Aaron wants to swim before dinner, so I get in the water. But the spasms get worse. I'm in excruciating pain, and when it moves up my diaphragm to my esophagus, I find it hard to breathe. Anyone who has this amount of pain would normally be on their way to a hospital. Actually, the first time I had this kind of pain, I ended up hospitalized overnight with a possible heart attack, but it turned out to be spasms of the digestive tract, including the esophagus. So now I just double over and bear it. I wander out to the Gazebo Bar and lie on one of the overstuffed love seats. The pain subsides immediately. This place is wonderful. I want to live here.

Aaron joins me, and we discuss moving to the coast for our last three months in Kenya. It makes sense since we have both fallen in love with the quaintness and coziness of the Swahili-influenced towns along the Indian Ocean.

I've been reading about the coastline's fascinating history of power struggles between Arab traders and Portuguese explorers. In almost every town along the coast, markets trade spices, coffee, and cotton as they did back then. On the ocean we have seen the iconic triangular sails of the *dhows,* vessels that were instrumental in shaping the area's economy, powered by the trade winds.

Aaron orders dinner for us. We indulge in comfort food, steak and mashed potatoes, served in the Gazebo Bar. After eating, I feel well, so we drive into the Tsavo East Park entrance past the foundation for the Visitor Center Project.

I say to Aaron, "I feel like we are going to see something spectacular tonight."

We round a curve and Aaron says, "Like this?"

A male impala stands within twenty-five feet of us. His family grazes behind him. I turn off the engine. They watch us, we watch them. All except one mother and baby eventually leave. She keeps inspecting us, and when Aaron looks off into the distance, she comes closer. She cautiously moves onto the dirt road in front of the car, never taking her eyes off us. Her baby follows. We only take pictures in our heads. Eventually they wander off into the bush.

Since joining the resort spa, we have seen five elephants from our spa perch. We have also seen Eurasian rollers, Egyptian geese, magpies, and starlings. Today we see five giraffes: two adults, two juveniles, and one baby. We feel so fortunate.

Aaron says we need to concentrate on getting car repairs and propane gas, paying our rent and utility bills, doing mail-outs, taking a Mombasa trip, and preparing for the upcoming Maasai wedding we have been invited to attend. All I can say is that our spa membership is good since I have prepaid. I have been taking money out of the ATM daily for food and necessities. Aaron accepts this and continues to pay the rent plus car and travel expenses. I want our adventure to be more of a partnership, and I have abandoned the idea of an all-inclusive experience for myself. Now that I have some control over my life and the decisions we make, I'm no longer feeling trapped in this amazingly beautiful land or in this relationship.

On Sunday we meet with four elders from the Waka Elephant tribe. Maintaining their culture is important to them, so we film their traditional dance, which depicts warriors hunting and women celebrating. Filming the dance of the elephant hunters makes us feel a little like tourists, even though we are doing this as photojournalists documenting their survival. They are appreciative. We treat ourselves to a nice candlelight dinner at the Red Elephant Lodge and see five elephants bathed in the red soils of Tsavo. Delightful.

One morning at the end of April, I motion for Katoo and Jasmine to come in for morning tea. I tell them that we are planning to leave Voi at the end of May. Katoo says he wants to keep Kasigau when we go back to the U.S. He will take her to his village, and she will get plenty of milks. This is all interpreted through Jasmine. What a sweet gesture.

I finish the second *Kasigau Conservationist* newsletter as Jasmine prepares lunch on the charcoal *jeko* (a three-legged traditional stove) since the propane burner is out of fuel. Because I have been so busy teaching, this newsletter is short with only two pages consisting of highlights and photos from our CIG workshop. I can't wait to find out what extraordinary happenings will precipitate new articles for the next quarterly issue, our final before completing our year in Africa. The winds are shifting.

A Slight Head Wind

*The real voyage of discovery consists not in seeing
new landscapes but in having new eyes.*

—Marcel Proust

May 2004
Voi, Kenya

O n May Day, Moses joins us for breakfast of mandazzis and coffee and asks if he might go to the coast
with us.

"What about your night job?" I ask.

He flicks his fingers and says, "No good."

So, it is decided: he'll go with us through August and
then home to see his family.

Moses is wearing Western attire today and looks smart
as he heads out to prepare for his brother's wedding.

Zachariah reminds us, "When you go to the wedding, you
will need to take pillows and blankets for it will be *baridi*."

I mention Hemmingway's last book, *True at First Light*.
I tell them how Hemingway wrote so much about the
Maasai.

Zachariah, deep in thought, adds, "I have heard the name, Ernest Hemingway, when I have sat with the elders listening to them share our tribe's history." The full moon is bright, and I stay out on the porch with the guys most of the evening. We play Mancala, an ancient game of stones, and Katoo thrashes me three times in a row.

In the morning Aaron grinds our last Java coffee beans for breakfast. Maybe the car will be fixed today and we will have time for a supply run to Mombasa before the wedding in Oloitokitok. Our salvation still remains the VWL for good food, peace and quiet, wildlife, and exercise.

Before we leave Voi for Mombasa, I can't find my debit or credit card. I realize that this is my only money in the whole wide world. Aaron shows up and sees me in my distress. I'm embarrassed. Then as I pull my passport out of my backpack, the cards pop out. Crisis averted. We finally get on the road to Watamu and my favorite hotel in all of Kenya, Hemingway's, on the Indian Ocean.

We search for a place to rent while visiting Turtle Watch and the Arocha Center. Houses for sale or rent have both Italian and Arab influences enhancing the African designs, and they are on some of the most beautiful beaches in the world. I'm determined to find a place. Aaron is wavering. I have to admit that they are too expensive, but I know we'll find a place. Sadly, we leave Watamu behind and continue on the coast road through a place called Vipingo. I stop some Kenyans who are walking along the roadside and ask them if they know of a place we might rent. They give us directions to a potential rental house on the oceanfront, Mrs. Jonas's farm.

We follow directions down a dirt road off the main highway where sugar and sisal plantations dominate the landscape. Mrs. Jonas is happy to meet us and takes us to see a house that she is renting on her property. It is old and charming: a whitewashed Swahili-style ranch with a thatched roof. Inside, the furniture is sparse and simple, old furniture that she says can be removed so that we might bring our own things from Voi. I can picture white curtains fluttering in the breeze and our wicker chairs out on the porch. I fall in love with the place immediately.

Mrs. Jonas invites us to make ourselves at home while she drives to town to sell the milk from her dairy cows. Aaron and I walk the beach. We watch fishermen lay their nets within the reef and clap to trap the fish inside.

After arriving with supplies from the nearest town, Mtwapa, Mrs. Jonas's cook, prepares a lunch of fish, fries, and salad for us. It takes us all afternoon to finalize the rental price: 30,000 ksh a month, a fair price. Then Mrs. Jonas suggests we buy the place, including her house and the dairy farm. Aaron agrees and asks me to be a part of this, not financially, but physically and emotionally. I'm not sure I can make such a commitment. I have a job waiting for me back home, a job I love. He tells her he'll get with his attorney and begin to make the necessary arrangements. She wants to see her land turned into a reserve. I feel like I'm playing out a scene from a movie, making these outlandish plans to buy land on the coast of Africa.

She tells us that there is a green mamba snake on the property as well as a twenty-foot python and a huge monitor lizard. I will encounter the green mamba and the monitor lizard during our time here, but, thank goodness, not the python. This place seems right in some ways and wrong in others. I need privacy. I hope I can have it here. This is supposed to be a time for the three R's: rest, relaxation, and reflection.

I notice that Aaron is falling asleep facing away from me these days. I follow suit. I wonder if he is thinking about going back to the U.S. I have a year's leave of absence and I'm not planning to return until the day I must report back to work. When I ask him why he's no longer showing me his mother's letters, he says that she's afraid that we're going to get married and I'll be using the family money for my own personal interests. I tell him that I'm not up for participating in securing Mrs. Jonas's property with him, so if that's why she's worried, there's no need.

Aaron goes to bed early, and I stay up writing and listening to the band at Free World.

Then a phone call comes. "Jambo."

"Moses, is that you?"

He hands the phone off to an English-speaker, who is with him, and this is what I learn: we will be leaving for the wedding next Sunday.

Before the wedding trip, I want to spend a day at the VWL and TDC. It will be relaxing to be with wildlife again. At the VWL we immediately see a male waterbuck and his five females at the watering hole while we are having lunch. First, I see his antlers moving above the weeds. They are adorned with vines and grasses, a regal sight. He's a large antelope distinguishable by the white pattern on the rump that we can see as he rises to a standing position. Next the females' ears protrude as they come out of the weeds onto the shoulder of the pond. His family drinks while he stands guard. I don't have the movie camera, but Aaron has his thirty-five mm. I will use this shot for next year's Christmas cards.

At TDC, Leigh said he had emailed us a couple of times. He has heard how successful the CIG class was in Voi and is anxious for his staff to participate. When he goes to make copies, he says, "Help yourselves to some coffee or tea." I guess if there were hard feelings about our leaving Rukanga, they have subsided. We discuss the CIG course I will be teaching to his staff in June. Leigh says that he will be a participant. I'm surprised; this should be interesting. We discuss the newsletter and what's happening at TDC and Origins Safaris.

When we leave at dusk, we see a giraffe by the edge of the road. As we approach, her baby hiding beside her becomes visible. The youngster is very inquisitive and stares at us. I'm able to get a shot with the long lens. As I turn to get the binoculars, the giraffes make their way into the bush, mother gaiting and baby jogging.

Moses calls again to confirm our trip on Sunday. Maasai Zachariah has agreed to watch over our place in Voi while we are gone. I wish he would change his mind and join us, but that is not likely. I never tire of seeing Zachariah, and when he arrives at our doorstep, I always say, "Where have you been? I have missed you."

A Wedding

*To improve the golden moment of
opportunity and catch the good that is within
our reach is the great art of life.*

—Samuel Johnson

*June 2004
Maasai Village, Kenya*

T he night before the wedding safari day, I'm so energized, I have trouble sleeping. Music is playing at
Free World all night. My stomach is upset. I'm thinking
about how Zachariah explained the engagement process: a
man gives goats, cows, and sugar to the girl's father as a
marriage proposal. This must be a girl from another clan
whom he has been interested in and vice versa. *Hopefully.*
The guy must be at least eighteen and the girl fifteen: both
are required to have been circumcised. I shudder at this
thought.

At 4:00 a.m., the wakeup call arrives. At 5:00 a.m., as
we're loading the car, I hear an awful sound, like an animal crying in distress. Aaron thinks it may be a goat
being slaughtered next door at Free World. If so, it's not

a painless death. Later, as we start to walk out our back gate, I look up and see a goat hanging from a tree with its throat slit. I immediately turn Aaron around, and we walk out through our front gate. *Life in Voi town. Life in Kenya. Life in Africa.*

Soon we are on the road, Kiyenni, Katoo, Aaron, and I. We must start out on the Taveta Road and stop at the police checkpoint. I'm driving, and the policeman approaches with a very stern look. Already I'm worried. I give him a big friendly smile to break the ice. He waves us on with a salute. We branch off to Chall Town then Churini Town and cross an old dilapidated bridge. The road, so far, has been narrow with large ditches on either side. When we arrive in Tamparare Town, we pick up Moses' brother and change drivers.

We've entered a sunflower plantation. Fields of great yellow blooms stretch out on both sides of the lane. I reach out and pick a small flower to put on the dashboard. Katoo reaches out of the back and picks several large ones. Suddenly, the clouds disappear to reveal snow-covered Mt. Kilimanjaro glistening on the horizon. Snow on the equator continues to amaze me. What a sight!

"Where be us? I ask.

The answer, "Tan-zan-ia."

Aaron and I shout, "Not Tanzania, our visas have expired."

But we receive this answer, "Hakuna matata! No border guards." Nonetheless, we are very happy to get back into

Kenya farther down the path. We continue to learn Maasai ways.

I find out that we are on our way to Kiyenni's boma first. A boma is a Maasai community corral with mud huts, called manyattas.

He looks at me and says, "Okay, Mama?"

I say, "Okay."

Kiyenni points to proceed straight. We are no longer on a road. We are in the bush once again, zigzagging along through the Acacia trees. Kiyenni is very excited, and so am I. We reach a small clearing with three huts encircled by a thorn fence. It is Kiyenni's home. He introduces us to his mother first. She is gracious. Kiyenni opens his pack, takes out a bag of hard candies and passes them out to several children who came running over when they heard the car. They are all adorable and want to shake hands with the muzungus. Kiyenni invites us to chi, tea with lots of milk. Aaron and I look to one another to see what we should do. I say a silent prayer that the water coming from an unknown source has been boiled properly. I ask for black tea since I'm lactose intolerant and, unlike Brazil, the milk here may not be *blessed*.

I decide that I should give a gift to Kiyenni's mama, so I run to the car and get a large canister of my favorite ginger snap cookies. I present it to her, and she is grateful.

The Mzee, the most respected elders, walk into the area where we sit under a large tree that provides shade in the hot, arid land. The tallest Maasai man seems to be the local leader. He has an attractive, noble face. He stands there, his eyes watching me calmly and attentively. The other men who come to say "Hi" are much impressed with my knowledge of their family names. I did my homework and even made family trees.

Towards the end of our visit, Kiyenni points to a young woman, who comes out of one of the huts, carrying a small child. This is Yolanda, his wife.

She keeps a close watch on me.

I give Kiyenni a gentle push, "Run to her, hug her, and kiss her."

He laughs and says, "Maasai, no kiss."

I take a picture of them with the digital, at least I thought I did, but upon downloading, it isn't there.

When tea is finished, we say our goodbyes.

Kiyenni looks at me and says, "Boma, good?"

"Yes, boma good."

Before loading up the car, Kiyenni quickly pulls another bag from his pack. It's medicine for one of his goats that's suffering from malaria. This is so touching.

We continue our journey to the wedding, crossing parched fields, empty riverbeds, and shallow valleys. Katoo points ahead of us, and there in a clearing is Moses, waving. I'm so relieved to see his smiling face. Moses greets us with handshakes and the women sing a song of greeting. They have a tradition to improvise a song and sing about those who have come from far away, wishing them safe journeys and a long life.

This boma has at least ten huts and a large area to hold their goats and cattle. Mama Moses comes out along with Moses's wife, Nasha, and places colorful necklaces and bracelets on Aaron and myself. In the Maasai culture red is the most important color and represents blood, the life force. Blue represents the sky that provides the water and rain for the cows, which are an important source of food. Green characterizes nourishment and production. Orange represents hospitality, warmth, friendship and generosity. Yellow is symbolic with fertility and growth. Our elegant jewelry made by his mama combines all the Maasai colors.

After the past two months of our Maasai language lessons, Aaron and I both go blank. I can't even remember "thank you" in Swahili let alone in Maa. The entourage leads us to the hut where we will be staying with Nasha and baby Moresia. Inside is almost pitch-black except for the thin streaks of sunlight slipping through the cracks in the mud. I only keep from tripping because I'm holding on to Aaron's belt in front of me. The interior, which is less than 100 square feet and without windows, is divided into three areas. A fireplace area sits right in front of the entrance. A woven partition wall divides the back half of the space into two sleeping areas. One, with a cowhide and a straw mat, is for Nasha and Moresia. Opposite is a second sleeping area with a single cot intended for visitors.

Back outside, we sit in the shade the hut provides and enjoy a Coca-Cola. John arrives in camp. I recognize him as the Maasai we passed earlier. He asked for a ride and we said, "No, too full!"

He is our interpreter for the day. *How embarrassing!*

Many of the elders are sitting around, some already drunk. Aaron begins photographing. I'm feeling very much alone. Then I am told that the bride's procession is coming from the next boma. I run for the movie camera and began shooting. The women sing several songs. The bride is beautifully adorned in a white dress decorated with blue, red, and yellow beadwork. She enters her mother-in-law's hut and stays in the hut all day. Several Maasai women attend to her. John asks, "Would you like to go in and visit with her?"

I hesitate at first but agree. As a guest of honor, I'm led in. The hut is dark except for a fire within three rocks that have been placed in the cooking area to create a sauna-like effect. She is sitting on the bed. I sit on the edge and take her hands in mine. She is crying though I'm not sure why. Then I see a tiny baby, around a month old, lying beside her. I have a camera with me. Light streams through a crack in the mud wall as I take a picture of her hands and a picture of her baby. I pat her hands again and leave the hut.

"She's extremely serious today and somewhat sad that she's leaving her village and her family," John tells me. "She can't talk today, but tomorrow she will be exceedingly happy. The baby is not hers. It's been placed there as an omen to improve the odds of bringing into being her own child."

Outside the boma, things are beginning to stir. The Maasai *morans* (warriors) are warming up for the dance. "Um-pa, um-pa," they chant, and they form a circle under the tree where our car is parked. Aaron and I climb up on the hood to photograph. We have been given permission to film at leisure. I'm very comfortable now and in the moment.

The jumping seems to go in rounds. Kiyenni is very good, maybe, the best. I look for Katoo. He is a bystander. I wonder why. He may be worried about his wife and daughter, who were reported to have been in the hospital with malaria but recently released. We've promised that when we leave the wedding, we'll take him home to Rombo and check on them. He starts to move closer into the circle and then pulls out his mirror and looks at himself. I can't help but laugh because all the warriors are so conscious of their appearance. I find them to be such a contradiction of terms. They are warriors who are never without their *pangas* (machetes and clubs) and ready for war but like women who fix their hair all the time, wear loads of jewelry, and are obsessed with their appearance.

The dance continues while the women sit under a tree in the distance having afternoon tea. As usual, I'm more comfortable being around the men, but I end up joining the women and share some of the photos I've taken. Eventually the dance moves inside the boma and the bride comes out of the hut.

Aaron and I have lunch with John in the field where the young warriors have grilled meat. We sit cross-legged, and

John carves the meat with his knife. I'm permitted to eat with the warriors because I'm a Western woman.

The dance continues, and this time Aaron joins in briefly. Maasai girls are now led into the middle of the circle, and the young warriors continue their dance. The more jewelry a young woman wears around her neck, the more she attracts attention and the higher the price she will fetch as a bride. The one thing that is taboo is for her to marry her boyfriends. Her father will choose her husband, and he will pick someone with a good reputation from another clan in another village, someone able to pay a high price.

At dusk, we take a group photo of Moses's family and then wait for the big dance. By now the elders, both men and women, are dropping like flies. Warriors carry a large woman away to one of the huts. Everyone is drinking a home-made brew that had to be ready before the wedding could begin. Others are snorting a weed. Many men are mimicking "suggestive" things to me, and one keeps coming after me and touching my hair. I hide behind Moses. Kiyenni and Katoo, who see my dilemma and tell me not to worry, since they are looking out for me.

Before dinner, we're invited into the hut of the newlyweds for gift–giving. We can't see the bride; she's back on the bed. The warriors choose a new name for her, one that means warrior. Then they present their gifts of a goat or a cow. Now it's our turn. Canisters for tea, coffee, and sugar aren't as impressive based on the reaction. We tried.

The goats and cows, led by a young boy, come into the boma at sundown with much fanfare and excitement. All activity stops to enjoy this happening. The dance never commences, much to my dismay, and there's no formal wedding ceremony. Around nine, Nasha serves a meal of potatoes and meat in soup made especially for us.

We're very tired so I grab our pillows, sheets, and blankets out of the car. Nasha, Moresia, Aaron, and I hit the sack while Moses stays up to watch the guests. He sits in our car, which has been pulled into the boma with the cattle. "For security purposes," he says.

Since purchasing the car, we've been providing a free service transporting locals to and from their jobs, to weddings and funerals, doctor's visits, and the weekly open-air markets. The vehicle has been invaluable for us and those we encounter along the way.

Tonight, we sleep in our clothes, and yes, we do sleep, but only after several tribal members peek in the hut to establish that we're actually staying in the manyatta.

∗

We awaken to a beautiful sunrise! People are passed out all over, and some are still drinking. I walk around and watch Moses' sister milk the goats. Then I play with Moresia and her friend in the bedroom. She puts the stamps I gave her on her forehead. We laugh. She climbs up on the bed, and I tickle her. I believe I have moved from square one to the winner's circle.

As I'm folding our sheets, Nasha is admiring them, so I gift them to her. Later I find her showing the linens to Mama Moses. Now I feel like I should give Nasha the matching pillowcases. She, surprised, holds her hands to her head, as I say, "This one is for Moses and this one is for you."

When I get back outside, Aaron is giving Moses his safari hat. Then we present the children with neck scarves. They run around the boma doing all sorts of things like pretending to be Batman with a cape or playing tug-of-war. The elders enjoy watching them. Moresia comes up to me and wants hers tied around her waist. The elders shout "Mama Moresia," so I tie it like a mama would wear, and she goes running off to show the women.

Katoo and Kiyenni show up, and we prepare for our journey. Moses looks sad. Aaron shakes his hand and puts 1000 ksh in it. He adds, "I'll have 350 wedding photos for you and your family."

Moses smiles, and I wince. "Really, 350 photos?" *What are you thinking, Aaron? We have only promised a few photos.*

Our interpreter, John, complains about a cut on his leg.

Moses comments to me, "John has big problem" and points to John's shin and then laughs his Moses laugh.

Aaron brings out some herbal cream. Soon after, John professes that the cream is making his leg much worse so he'll need a ride back to his village. Some of the elders see the cream and ask for it to be put on their cut heads from falling drunk in the night. Aaron provides it on their fingers so that they might rub it in.

A mama elder grabs me and asks for something for her eyes. I bring her some eye drops. I do not put them in but try to show her how to do it. I sincerely hope they help.

Exhausted and exhilarated, both at the same time, we gather ourselves and slowly depart this amazing scene. We wave and yell, *"Ole seri!"* and proceed into the shade of Kilimanjaro.

In the Shade of Kilimanjaro

*Kilimanjaro is a snow-covered mountain 19,710 feet
high, and it is said to be the highest mountain in
Africa. Its western summit is called the Masai 'Ngaje
Ngai', the House of God.*

—Ernest Hemingway, "The Snows of Kilimanjaro"

June 2004
Rombo, Kenya

Rombo is our first destination and I can see that Katoo
is anxious to check on his wife and child. I look back
at him in the car. He has his face in his hands like he's about
to cry.

I say, "Where to?"

"The hospital."

I learn the mother and daughter became ill in the night
and had to return to the hospital. Katoo goes into the hospital clinic. The hospital administrator tells Katoo that his
four-year-old daughter has tuberculosis and needs to go to
the Oloitokitok Hospital for treatment.

The young child coughs a few times on the way. Since
I'm driving, I can only glance back at her for a moment.

but I do notice that she has Katoo's bright, dark-brown eyes.

Katoo checks his young daughter into the tuberculosis section of the hospital and we are instructed to depart. It is hard for us to leave this young child alone but at least her mother will be able to visit with her.

Hemmingway's *True at First Light* features Oloitokitok, a border town between Tanzania and Kenya at an elevation of 8,000 feet. We don't have much time to look around, but I do notice a nicely landscaped guesthouse called Kibo Slopes. It's a starting point for those planning to climb Mt. Kilimanjaro.

The road to Amboseli National Park is twenty-four kilometers on the dirt highway. It's a crude path, much of it under construction. After several hours, we're finally in the park. Immediately I see a couple of large greyish-black animals in the distance. After a moment with the binoculars, I'm able to identify them as wildebeests, an African antelope with a long head, a beard and mane, and a sloping back. From then on, we see a large array of these strange looking but magnificent animals. They have stripes on their hindquarters and their large heads are out of proportion to their bodies. I'm not aware that they will be on a mass migration in a few months. We make our way to the Amboseli Serena Lodge. It's a sorely needed, well-deserved oasis for a hot shower, change of clothes, nourishment, and sleep. I believe this is the first time the guys have stayed in a park lodge in their own country.

The morning brings adventure for me. Out of bed early, I dress and make my way to the veranda. I flush a covey of guinea fowl out of the bushes, at least fifty. I find a coffee bar, Java, no less, and begin to enjoy my beverage at a table on the patio. As I watch a herd of wildebeest, monkeys begin to surround me. I'm enjoying them when I hear footsteps from behind. It's a Maasai guard with his, *a-moody* (stick) chasing them away.

So many hotels will hire a Maasai to act as a security guard or as a tourist attraction since they are the only tribe to truly retain their cultural ways. We chat for a while, me in broken Maa and he in broken English. Eventually he's called to the reception area.

When the waiter approaches me, she says, "The Maasai told me you speak his language." She's impressed.

The guys and Aaron finally meet me for breakfast in the Twiga room. Kiyenni can't find the sugar. I show him the yellow packets and give him two. He starts to put the packets down in his coffee. I yell stop and show him how the sugar is stored inside the package. He's surprised and we all enjoy the sugar packet lesson.

Walking back to the room, I see Katoo standing by the pool. I can't resist pretending I'm going to push him in. He catches his balance and then laughs. He's very surprised that Mama would do such a thing.

While we're loading the car, a monkey jumps in the front seat.

I yell, "There's a monkey in the car."

It gets scared and jumps out with a travel tissue holder. The monkey, sitting up on an overhead beam, looks inside, finds dirty tissues, and throws them down before running away. I have it all on video.

We drive out of the park and to a secondary road. Kiyenni and Katoo look at the map and indicate that it's the Oloitokitok-Nairobi Highway. I want to turn right and go through Tsavo West National Park to the Lava Flow area to Voi, but they talk me out of it, saying it can't be done. We go left and almost end up almost in Nairobi. Now it's over 300 kilometers back to Voi. I'm glad the hotel packed a box lunch for us. The guys even eat the chicken (ku ku) drumsticks.

*

We have promised Katoo another trip to Oloitokitok to check on his daughter. Our time in the Tsavo area is running out, so we combine Tsavo West National Park with our trip to Oloitokitok. Aaron and I are up early. We get on the road at daybreak with three passengers: Katoo and his two brothers. The youngest, one of my favorites, a twenty-three-year-old who is torn between his culture and Western ways, has either lost his job at the railroad station or has quit. I lose many of the details in the language differences. But he's going back home to find a wife, I suspect. The other one is headed home to see his wife and child.

We see this as a good opportunity to take the guys through the national park.

On the way to the Mito Andrei Gate we see a dead lion on the side of the road. I'm tempted to stop and take a photo, but it's badly bloated. We proceed to the gate. We explain that we will be taking two Maasai to Oloitokitok and leaving them, then coming back to the park and staying the night at the Lodge. A police officer wants a lift over to our exit gate, Chyulu. He climbs in the back and becomes our tour guide, directing us to Mzumi Springs. He explains that this water comes from the Chyulu Hills and serves Voi on the way to Mombasa. I remember hearing about this water in the movie, *Out of Africa.*

We pass several small pools as we walk along the rudimentary trail, and we are excited to spot hippos, crocs, birds, fish, monkeys, and baboons. We drive on to the Shetani Lava area and are amazed again. A small antelope is camouflaged on the volcanic rock. I want to stay longer, but we need to get to the hospital in Oloitokitok.

Upon leaving the Chyulu gate, we learn we will need an armed guard to continue. Our passenger count goes up to seven. The trip takes two and a half hours. And the highlight is a mother cheetah and her three juveniles who cross the road in front of us. They are the fastest mammals on earth, but today they stride in slow motion. Spectacular!

At the hospital, Katoo is anxious to see his daughter. We walk back to the tuberculosis center, a compound of small dilapidated huts. Katoo's daughter is sitting on a stump with the most pathetic look on her face. Katoo looks for his wife, ignoring his daughter at first. She does not get up and run or walk over to him.

I say, "Katoo, there she is."

He finally walks over to her and puts his hand on her head, the Maasai way of respect. He has a yellow T-shirt we picked up at the visitor center gift shop. I want him to give it to her but he says, "The mama has to do that."

Katoo is quite upset that no family member is here with his daughter. We are told they have gone to town. His sweet baby is left alone, looking abandoned and traumatized. We decide to go to town to look for the family. I tell him to explain to his daughter so that she will understand that we will be coming back. He misunderstands and thinks I mean for him to bring her with us. I'm glad it happened that way. As we walk to the car, he places his hand on her head again and then finally holds her hand. They talk some but very little.

I have Katoo sit with his daughter in the front seat. He wipes her runny nose with tissues I give him since I have been told that TB is highly contagious, the reason patients are kept in a secluded area on the hospital grounds.

Once we find Kays, her mother, we return to the hospital. Katoo's daughter must stay two months, and it will cost 800 ksh a week. I have already agreed to pay. She still has not received her present. Finally, Katoo decides that it's time to go. He puts the T-shirt on his little girl. She is a bit more responsive but still looks so forlorn.

We fly down the road, pick up our guard, and make it to the park entrance and to our hotel on time. Aaron gets us a suite, a place one could live in. We also have this wonderful veranda overlooking the watering hole, where we see water buffalo, impala, waterbuck, hyenas, baboons, birds, and a baby giraffe.

We say, "*Lala Salama*," (good night) in another four-poster bed surrounded by netting. We don't get wound up in it tonight. We are too tired.

Aaron and I get up at five o'clock and go to the veranda to await sunrise. We hope the baby giraffe lived through the night, despite the stalking hyenas. After breakfast we're on the move and must exit the park by nine o'clock. Aaron drives like a mad man. I can see my stepfather in him. The last time I agreed to ride with my stepfather, I was sixteen years old. He drove like a maniac, taking me to work at my summer lifeguarding job. Upon arrival, I got out of the car, slammed the door, and vowed to never get in a car with him again. And I never did.

Aaron and I get lost. We will never exit by nine, so I convince him to slow down and enjoy the park. We follow the Tsavo River and encounter hippos. Katoo is learning how to operate the digital camera, and he photographs Aaron and me with the hippos in the background.

When we return home, Moses is back. The wedding took its toll. He has been sick and has lost weight. Stomach problems, he contends. He says that Moresia talks about the mama with the sweets and the school papers. I'm glad she remembers me.

Voi remains the same: Rooster has the first word in the morning, next is the Muslim call to prayer, then the birds, next is a toss-up. Will it be a Maasai at the gate? Or the morning drumming of the pipes after the water is turned on at six? Or the scrape of Jasmine's door on the concrete as she exits to start her day's chores. On our best days, we have *khowa* (coffee) on the porch before the sun get too bright.

My Heart is Africa

You woke up in the morning and thought: Here I am,
where I ought to be.

—Isak Dinesen (Karen Blixen), Out of Africa, 1937

June 2004
Nairobi, Kenya

We are in Nairobi once again for another CIG class. This is a great class; we laugh so much. The participants catch on very quickly, so we have time to experiment with a two-minute speech using tangibles and intangibles. They are true storytellers. Safari guide Leroy has us in stitches when he relays his most amusing experience:

> *I'm out with two clients on a game drive using my hand-held microphone in my Land Rover to keep them posted on wildlife that I see up ahead. I spot a giraffe nursery, a common way for giraffes to watch their young while they forage in the high trees. This will be great. As I drive slowly forward not wanting to spook the animals, I look in my rearview mirror. **Where are my clients?** All I can*

see is a baboon sitting on the top of the car seat where my clients had been sitting. I panic. **Where are they? I don't see them or hear them? When did they get out of the car?** *I hit the brakes and come to an abrupt halt. As I'm jumping out of the car, I'm yelling at the baboon, "Get out of here!" The baboon, startled, leaps into the air and runs off into the bush. I look back down the road thinking my clients must be behind on the car track. There is no sign of them. Then out of the corner of my eye, I see strands of blonde hair blowing in the breeze. When I get closer, I see my clients scrambling up from the floorboards where they had taken refuge."* **Thank God they are safe.**

By Thursday evening, Aaron and I are checking the written tests and making participation certificates. I tell Aaron that something is wrong with me. My body is out of balance. My belly spasms in agony, and I understand what is coming next. Eventually, the dry heaves set in and I'm dehydrated. The only option is a taxi to Nairobi Hospital. Acute food poisoning is the diagnosis. The ER staff isn't very friendly. It's a rough night.

At six in the morning a cab sent by Aaron arrives to pick me up, but there is no way I can leave. I'm supposed to video and grade all the oral presentations for our last day of class. Aaron shows up around eight panicked. "I have checked you out."

He's desperate, but I'm still nauseated.

Dr. Roy stops by the ER and says, "I'm checking her into the hospital."

Aaron leaves and holds the class on his own. He videos and grades the participants. *Thank you, Aaron.* One of the participants, Albanus, shows up at the hospital to check on me. He says all the guys wish they could have come to see me. I'm glad they didn't come since I look so bad. He misses giving his presentation. I'm so sorry.

At noon I feel a little better and ask for Jell-O. The hospital staff is excellent and makes Jell-O for me even though I can't keep it down. I've been given something in a drip that's making me nauseated again. They take it out, and I'm better but need to spend the night. I know I need one more day to recoup, but I'll have to leave for Voi in the morning since we're preparing to move to Vipingo.

Aaron has finalized our move. New Generations will transport all our belongings to our new home for 5000 ksh. When we all arrive in Vipingo the next day, it's raining. They unload our stuff and ask to be paid the 50,000 ksh they say was agreed upon. Aaron is irate. They argue for hours with no one giving in. I'm just a bystander who's still not feeling well. Eventually, the movers leave with only 5000 ksh which is less than $100.

On our second day on the coast, I decide to make a run to Nyali for things like bottled water and groceries. Aaron is not feeling well enough to accompany me, so we decide Katoo should go along. When we left Voi, I didn't get a chance to say *"Ole seri"* to Zachariah, and this left me feeling uneasy.

Today I'm worried about Katoo and wonder if he's going to be lonely here on the coast. I tell him we saw a couple of Maasai walking along the road as we drove south last night.

Katoo and I are cruising with all the windows down. When I hear "Jambo-Jambo" playing on the radio, I turn up the volume and let it blast from the speakers. This is the latest hit song by the African Safari Band. Katoo and I sing along. The little town of Mtwapa has a road with the largest potholes I've seen so far. Suddenly Katoo yells, "Kiyenni!" I'm just about to enter the worst of all potholes when Kiyenni comes running over. It's all so exhilarating. Then much to my surprise, Zachariah jumps out of the shadows. Now I'm even more thrilled. Once again Africa has a way of making sure nothing is left unsaid.

Traffic is at a standstill behind me with horns sounding off. I finally find a place to pull over out of the flow. Maasai friends of friends quickly surround us. Kiyenni and Zachariah climb in, and we head to the Nakumatt, what I call the Japanese Walmart. We shop, and when we are finished, I suggest we all go to Pizza-Pizza for cokes. Here I am with three handsome Maasai warriors drinking sodas and celebrating our good fortune. We are definitely attracting attention from the waiters and customers. Zachariah says, "Cheers," and we clink bottles.

This is Zachariah's first trip to the coast, so we head over to the public beach.

The sky and the ocean are gray after two days of storms. Huge amounts of seaweed have washed in, but we walk out into the water anyway. We run and chase an ocean liner on the horizon.

Zachariah walks with me and says how happy he is to be here on our little safari. He mentions my smile that 'draws him in.' His muscular body and intelligence draws me in. Unfortunately, the guys need to get back to Voi to work tonight and need a matatu. I drive them as far into Nyali as I can and find them a ride.

On the way home, Katoo and I go back to La Veranda for dinner and more shopping. We order extra food to take home to Aaron and Moses. This has been an incredible day for Maasai Mama.

Once we're settled in our new place, we begin to explore the coast. When the tide is out, we walk miles away from the house, stepping carefully, picking up strange shells. The coast below the house has a row of scooped-out deep caves. When the tide comes in, the water rises to the level where our house is built. The high waves run up the bank and crash into the wooden bench that sits on the point, or into us if we stay out too long.

On our tenth day, I'm up early and have made a pot of coffee. We all have colds except Katoo. He's on night watch. He enjoys the plate of cookies and the coffee that I share with him. I'm so far behind on writing the last of our newsletters for the Conservation Trust that it's hard to know where to start. We have approximately six weeks left in Africa, and now the pressure is on. I still have so many places I want to go, so many things left to see and do, and so many people to meet.

Our schedule is crazy. Two of our remaining weeks will be spent teaching CIG classes, one in Nairobi and the other at TDC. Plus, we have a visitor, my cousin, coming for one week in July. In August I'm especially looking forward to covering the ceremony for the grand opening of the Lumo Community Wildlife Sanctuary. I have trained their staff and worked with the organizers throughout the year. Writing a story for *SWARA* magazine and the *Kasigau Conservationist* will complete all the commitments I've made for the year's stay in Kenya. And I still want to take that trip to Rwanda to see the mountain gorillas and visit the island of Lamu.

Aaron and I continue to have peak experiences when we have focus and purpose, like teaching the CIG courses, or writing the "Kasi Mews" part of the newsletter, or exploring the coast. In all of these moments, we're able to find comic relief that erupts into the most glorious laughter.

Aaron and I decide it would be fun to write a children's book based on Kasi's adventures in Africa. We come up with ideas like *Kasi Is In Heat or Kasi's Rite of Passage* since we are taking her on a road trip to Mombasa to have her spayed. We begin to draw illustrations of a car driving down the highway with Kasi looking out the back window at a multitude of male cats running after her behind the car.

But we also experience valleys. We endure the heat and transportation woes. We navigate financial stressors. I have to constantly remind Aaron to wire home for funds and/or to take his meds.

I try to spend as much of my free time as possible with the guys, documenting their culture through photos and videos. Aaron doesn't seem to be on board for this and leaves me a message on the computer one morning.

How you spend so much time with the Maasai for inter-pretive 'whatever' is driving me nuts. This also drives me apart from you. We should be building bridges instead of comfortable walls. So, work on yourself and then we can work together.

This angers me. Is he gaslighting me? I just want to take advantage of the time we have left to learn more about the Maasai culture.

*

Today we must leave for Nairobi for our third Origins CIG Class. We are up at half past four and ready and packed three hours later. Aaron is ready to go, but I'm not. I'm recuperating from an upper respiratory infection, and I have never felt this disorganized in all my life.

My body is still off balance from the food poisoning and now the cold or maybe "a little malaria." I'm very tired. After jumping in the car, I remember that I forgot the map for Tsavo East National Park. I run back into the house for it and run back out. I'm holding up the map for

Aaron to see, and before I know what is happening: I'm on the ground after tripping and hitting my knee on some coral rock. I jump up immediately in excruciating pain. I feel like I have a piece of coral in my kneecap. The Maasai come running to help me, but Aaron never gets out of the car. We proceed, even though I need ice. Even more, I need fresh air so I don't pass out. The trip is unpleasant to say the least. Aaron is falling asleep driving in the park. When we go to switch places, I hit my kneecap on the dashboard. Once again, I'm nauseated from the agonizing pain, but I'm able to drive the rest of the way to the Voi Wildlife Lodge. Upon arrival, all I want to do is to be left alone in the room to nurse my wounds.

In the morning I'm once again sociable and we head into Nairobi but the thought of spending five or six days at the Boulevard Hotel after last time's experience will be a challenge. It's interesting that neither Aaron nor I ever got sick with food poisoning when we lived in the bush or consumed food in the Maasai villages.

The class has only four guides. We'll be able to leave them on their own and do business in Nairobi. The first day we walk down to the Norfolk Hotel. In the gift shop I'm drawn to an elephant sculpture, and Aaron spies an artfully-carved giraffe with a baby. We can't resist making these rather extravagant purchases. We meander over to the Java House and delight in cappuccinos. Felix from the first CIG class is there with clients for a safari. He finds me and gives me the biggest bear hug, lifting me off the ground.

"We were all so worried about you."

We go on to KWS Orphanage to see the lion cubs that I've heard so much about.

Later we are permitted to enter the cage for photos with three beautiful babies. I thank the keepers with 1000 ksh. In the gift shop we buy KWS brand clothing to take home for family and friends.

Our CIG class ends early on Thursday and we make a trip to Voi to check on our mail. When I look out the door of the post office, I see Kiyenni, and he sees me. We head towards one another. I have wanted to give Kiyenni a hug for a long time. He gives me a great smile and says, "Oh, Mama!" After hugging, we go back to the traditional handshake.

Aaron says, "I think Kiyenni would take you as his wife in a heartbeat."

"Well, he does not have enough cows to cover my bride price," I laugh.

We are in Voi maybe for the last time. Kiyenni exclaims, "There's Zachariah."

I excitedly rush across the street to meet with him. Zachariah tells us he's now jobless.

I blurt out, "We can take you home with us." But I add, "We'll only be around for another six weeks."

He says he understands and I say, *"Ole seri, stay in peace."*

We continue our errands and I'm feeling sad. Out of the blue, Aaron says, "Let's take him," and so the hunt begins.

The Maasai have a great network, and Zachariah receives the message. We offer him a job but say that he must be ready to leave in the morning.

After spending the night at TDC, we return to get him. He has no suitcase or duffle bag, just what he is wearing and a thin blanket over his shoulders to ward off the coolness of the morning. He carries a pouch holding his ID card and a small amount of money under his shuka. I'm amazed at how the Maasai are able to travel so lightly when we have backpacks and suitcases for all our stuff.

The next day in Vipingo, Zachariah says, "Mama's heart was broken. Now she is happy."

The Incident

The more I traveled, the more I realized that fear
makes strangers of people who should be friends.

—Shirley MacLaine

July 2004
Watamu, Kenya

The Ruins of Gede are a historical and archaeological site near the coast of Kenya on the Indian Ocean. The ruins are inland from Watamu and down a winding track through encompassing overgrowth. It is said that the people living here were a thriving but oddly secretive community hidden away in a semi-jungle setting along the coast between Malindi and Mombasa. The Muslim inhabitants traded with other people from all over the world for centuries. Sea travel was common. The site is adjacent to the town of Gede, within the Arabuko-Sokoke Forest. This woodland area is characterized by tropical dry forest within a montage of savannas, grasslands, and wetlands.

I maneuver our Land Cruiser slowly through this seaside jungle. The twisted branches resemble ghostly arms

that appear to come alive and close in on us. I have diffi-
culty following the car track winding through the tangle of
vegetation. I'm looking for light at the end of the tunnel,
but there is none in sight. The vines dangle in front of us
and to the sides, brushing against the body of our car. The
odor floating on the atmosphere wafts its way into our vehicle and reminds me of driving through a town in the U.S.
that has a paper factory. This scent mixes with the stench
of roadkill rotting in a ditch along the highway. I place my
right hand over my mouth and nose to no avail. I can take no
more and bring the car to a stop.

Chills rack my body. "There is something terribly
wrong here." I want to turn around and abandon our sightseeing for the day.

I tell Aaron but he just laughs and says, "You are the one
who wanted to come here and begged me to come along. So
just proceed."

Even though his amusement doesn't sit well with me,
I continue on. Eventually, the jungle opens to a significant
clearing, and we find a parking area in front of a small visitor center. A friendly tour guide, Mohammed, greets us.
He's the only person manning this place. When he insists,
we sign the guest register, I become apprehensive and immediately note that we are the only ones signed in for today and actually, the only ones who have signed in for an
entire week. My anxiety grows. This is not like me. I love
new adventures, especially ones that stimulate the adrenal
glands.

Mohammed takes us on a quick tour of this primeval forested site. This inner walled town reveals remnants of mosques, a great palace, and numerous one-story houses all made from stone. An outer wall contains large open areas that originally contained earth and thatch houses. Monkeys run along the ruined walls, discreetly keeping an eye on us. The site still seems to half belong to the jungle.

Aaron is bored with the tour and heads back to the visitor center with Mohammed, who seems enthralled with the opportunity to interact with an American. I browse alone through the ancient town, striding along the low-walled areas and think about the uncomfortable imaginary walls building up between Aaron and I.

The brochure I'm reading states that from this Swahili coastal settlement gold, ivory, slaves, ebony, mangrove poles, copper, copal gum, frankincense, myrrh, and crystal rock were exported. The trade winds in the Indian Ocean, as well as the relatively short distances between landmasses, facilitated maritime trade along the coast of East Africa.

With its numerous Arab inhabitants, the town became wealthy and reached its peak in the fifteenth century as a center of trade. But the last families left the town during the first half of the seventeenth century for unknown reasons. I'm besieged with chills again.

I hightail it back to the visitor center, where I find Aaron and Mohammed playing a game of checkers.

I beg Aaron, "Please let's go."

"Hon, we are playing the best two out of three. Just relax."

I look around the small gift area and coyly motion Mohammed over to the sales area so that I can purchase a tiny handmade drum and maybe end their game. But he eagerly returns, and I find myself waiting again.

Finally, Aaron is ready to leave. I yell thank you to Mohammed and jump into the driver's seat of the Land Cruiser in hopes of a quick exit.

As I navigate a curve in the car track, I see a single bicycle tire rolling towards us. I slow down. A young girl around nine or ten years old in a faded pink dress chases after the tire with a stick. This is not the first time I've seen a child playing with a tire in this manner during our time in Kenya. But the tire veers off the path and lands in a ditch. As it does, she looks back where I can see a younger child, a boy, lying in the middle of the road. He has obviously tripped and fallen.

A man comes running out of the tangled scrub on the side of the road and picks the child up in his arms. As he does, one of the child's blue flip-flops falls off. Aaron sees the sandal and asks me to come to a full stop to let them retrieve it.

I motion for the man to go ahead. Instead he walks up to my open window and asks me to take the child to the hospital. The small boy, age five or six, is bleeding over one eye. It doesn't look serious enough to equate this with an emergency. I'm ready to move on and get out of here.

Then I hear Aaron say, "Yes."

Aaron jumps out and lifts the hatchback. "You can get in here."

The man places the child in the middle of the back and then disappears back into the bush. The boy sits alone crying, and Aaron and I look at each other in disbelief. We both agree we will not transport this young boy without an adult.

Local villagers appear from the shadows of the forest as if they've been hiding behind the trees all along. Aaron seeks to find an adult to accompany the child, but everyone is shouting and closing in on us. I see what's happening. Everyone thinks we have hit the boy with our car. More people arrive, and no one is willing to get in the car. I find myself yelling to be heard over the crowd. I'm not sure anyone understands me, but I keep yelling. The car is still running and I am ready to make a quick departure. Aaron is still clueless and acting like the normal, caring person he is.

I whisper, "They think we've hit the boy. We need to get out of here now."

Suddenly three or four children climb in the back. Aaron removes them. The crowd builds. I scan the facial expressions of the loudest most vocal demonstrators. Their lips take on lethargic movements as I attempt to read them. Then out of the surrounding jungle foliage the original man creeps back onto the scene. Aaron ushers him into the vehicle.

I shout to Aaron, "Shut the door!"

I honk the horn. The crowd, still shouting and pointing fingers, moves back so we can pass.

I shriek to the man, "Give me directions to the hospital."

He points to the main road.

We unload the man and child in the parking lot of the hospital and immediately make ourselves scarce.

A mile or so down the road we realize that we're still not breathing properly after the precarious position we found ourselves entangled in. Then I remember we have left our names and address at the Gede Ruins guest register. We can be found, tracked down, and wrongly accused. The man we transported with the child has thanked us, but did he really see what happened? And if so, will he tell the truth or was he a part of a plan?

Later in the evening we visit Paul and Lynn, our USAID friends, and Paul says, "No good deed goes unpunished." I have never heard this before and find the idea troubling. They tell us horror stories of others in similar situations. Paul thinks we may have been set up.

When I continue to tell how I got chills while touring the Gede site, Lynn shares why people in the expat community do not enter it. The Gede indigenous forest is a sacred site for traditional rituals and sacrifices for the local Giriama, one of the Mijikenda tribes. Each Mijikenda clan has their own sacred place known as *kaya*, a shrine for prayer, sacrifices and other religious rituals. Kayas are located deep in the forests, and it is considered taboo to cut the trees and vegetation around them. Due to the kaya taboo, the forest regions around the Mijikenda kayas have remained untouched for many years. However, people have started destroying these kaya forests to make way for agriculture, buildings, and tourism activities. This forced the government and conservation agencies to institute measures for protecting the biological diversity found in the kayas by declaring them national monuments. The Mijikenda people maintain a community that surrounds the Gede ruins. They believe that evil and ancestral spirits reside at Gede and will harm anyone who trespasses.

Happy to arrive home safely, I see that my Maasai friends have already heated bath water for me. What a nice surprise. I slip into the tub, finally stop shivering, and try to wash away the events of the day.

Final Goodbyes

I will remember Africa, but will Africa remember me?

—Karen Blitzen

August 2004
Lumo Wildlife Sanctuary, Kenya

A plaque at the Lumo Community Wildlife Sanctuary reads: *This camp was officially opened by Mr. William M. Bellamy, Ambassador of the United States of America on the 4th of August 2004.*

Aaron and I are here photographing and preparing for the ribbon-cutting ceremony. With us is Maasai Moses, the only Maasai at this Taita tribal event. Ambassador Bellamy acts out a scene where he places an animal skin across his shoulder and kneels down holding a spear.

A Taita storyteller gives an oral presentation called Waiting for the Maasai:

> *The Taita People feared the Maasai greatly because the*
> *Maasai, the protectors and owners of all the cattle on*

earth, would come and steal the cattle from the Taitas. Back in the day, the Maasai did not consider this stealing, because all the cattle already belonged to them, according to god's plan. The Taita would wait crouched low behind their animal shields with bows and poisoned arrows ready. Sometimes they would have to wait all day in this position.

Ambassador Bellamy sees Maasai Moses in the audience and points out that today the Taita do not have to wait long. Everyone looks at Moses in his red shuka with his beaded ear fobs. What a surprise. Laughter erupts. The scene is set for rejoicing when drums sound off near the main gate and Taita dancers make their way up the hill to the amphitheater.

A young rogue elephant is visible roaming around behind the stage. Even though we went rogue ourselves, Aaron and I have now completed our last commitment to the Taita Discovery Center's Wildlife and Community Participation Programs through Origins Safaris. I'm proud of what we have contributed, but I know I've gained so much more than I've given. *Thank you, Africa. Thank you, Kenya. Thank you, Taita. Thank you, Maasai.*

I haven't forgotten about Lamu Island, another one of the Muslim settlements on the coast. It has stayed in my mind for all these months, and I'm not going to leave without visiting. Lamu, a small island of mangroves, is a UNESCO World Heritage Site and the oldest and best-preserved Swahili settlement in East Africa. I look forward to seeing Lamu's architecture, with its influences from Europe, India, and Arabia. Donkeys still carry loads through the narrow alleyways since no cars are allowed except one for the sultan. I had also promised Maasai Katoo he would have the opportunity to join us if we were to go in another bush plane.

When booking the trip to Lamu, I see a brochure on Fort Jesus showcasing lighted torches in the night. I immediately book the tour for my cousin Walt and myself. Walt will be visiting after his walking safari in the Maasai Mara. Aaron does not want to join us. He doesn't tell me why, and I don't ask.

Walt is waiting at the airport in Malindi when I arrive. Aaron calls and suddenly decides to join us, so we stop back in Vipingo to pick him up. We run into Mrs. Jonas. After proper introductions, she surprises me and looks directly at cousin Walt. "Aaron is going to buy my land and turn it into a reserve," she says.

Walt is surprised and adds, "That's a great idea. It's beautiful here."

Aaron says, "We really need to get on the road to Mombasa."

*

In Mombasa we sail on an old wooden ship, and the warm night winds carry us out of the harbor to catch the incredible sunset. It's awesome. Next, we head further out to sea to Fort Jesus. We dock and walk through Old Town past the original slave market to the inner fort, where several Arabs dressed in white gowns and carrying fire torches lead us through a dark tunnel down to a small auditorium for the sound and light show. The music is inspiring, and the lights and slides are a valiant attempt at working with the latest technology to highlight the history of the fort.

Tables are set up outside on a patio. They hold large candelabras and tablecloths featuring a cross. We dine in the moonlight of an evening sky.

Aaron says, "I can feel old souls present here."

The following day we fly to the island of Lamu and Katoo is understandably nervous. He is forced to give up his *runga*, a club that all Maasai warriors carry with them. The attendant promises to return it after we land. Katoo is reluctant, but he concedes and takes his seat. I'm having fun filming it all to show to his family when we return.

After departing the plane, we board a boat for a short trek to Lamu island. In the distance we see its minarets reaching high in the sky towards Allah. We aren't there one minute before Katoo sees another Maasai.

Exploring the island on foot takes us all afternoon. We wind through the narrow streets and pass intricately, carved, wooden doorways. We draw a crowd of men in their long robes, and children with beautiful, dark brown eyes stare at us as they play in the streets with their homemade toys. The people here are incredibly friendly and allow us to browse in their shops peacefully.

At sunset we can hear the muezzin's last call to prayer for the day. I can't explain how it touches my soul every time I've heard this call during the year I've lived in Africa, but it draws me in every time. Today is no exception. I sit in silence on the balcony as the gentle sound comes whispering through the colorful shutters.

We spend an unforgettable evening together, listening to the murmurings of the evening tide as it gently reaches for the sea wall. In the morning we head to the magnificent Chela beach for a swim. Katoo stays on land secured in a hammock. He seems to enjoy watching us splash and frolic in the still waters. The champagne brunch at the Pineoyn Hotel is an exquisite and perfect ending to our time in this remote, peaceful corner of the African continent.

A few days later Zachariah and I take Walt back to the Malindi Airport for his departure. I see a young boy with a Maasai headdress of ostrich feathers. It's original and catches my eye. Zachariah sees me looking at it and says that he can get me a more beautiful one from his village.

He puts one of his brothers in charge of finding the leather piece. His sister will restore the beadwork, and then Zachariah will have to enter Amboseli National Park to pick up ostrich feathers for the adornment. I worry because the Maasai are banned from the park since, in the past, young warriors proved their manhood by entering and killing a lion. They can and have entered with us before since they were acting as our tour guides. I decide to leave this decision up to Zachariah.

The next stop on our farewell tour is Rombo, Katoo's home. They are waiting for us on Sunday. Mama greets us, and in turn, we give gifts of *sucare* (sugar), biscuits, and children's clothing. I don't even recognize his daughter, Racia, because this child looks so healthy and happy. I'm glad we've had the opportunity to see her healed from tuberculosis. I play the video of Katoo climbing the steps of the bush plane as it was getting ready to fly us to Lamu. Katoo is full of pride for his accomplishment.

Mama Katoo presents me with a string of beads. I'm almost in tears. Kays, Katoo's wife, presents Aaron with a beautiful necklace. He is also touched with their generosity. We end our visit with hugs and goodbyes in Maa.

While driving back to the coast, I ask Zachariah about the string of beads Mama Katoo had given me. Zachariah explains that these beads are made by the mama to be used to adorn her children in celebration of circumcisions, lion kills, and *Enuto*, when a warrior becomes an elder. These beads have adorned Katoo and his siblings as they have progressed through life's stages. The black and white beads are rare and very expensive, and there are many. I'm honored.

The guys then present me with the ostrich feather headdress. They've done a fantastic job of making it special. They tell me how they found male and female feathers to adorn the mask. This is a mask traditionally worn during a warrior's lion hunt. I love it. They have fun modeling and pretending they are stalking a lion.

Going back to Voi is sad because we have so many friends to say goodbye to. I hope we will all be lifelong friends. As we drive away from the Tsavo Park Hotel, Kiyenni says his final goodbye by raising his stick high in the air like a salute. He holds it there until we are out of sight.

Jasmine invites us to her home in Rukanga to meet her father. We arrive late afternoon and find out they have been waiting all day for us. Jasmine has prepared dinner. When Jasmine's mama sees me, she comes rushing towards me and we shake hands until I feel like my arm might drop off. Then we laugh and laugh and shake hands some more. It's so hilarious. She is so happy.

On the way out of the village, we visit the banda for the last time and deliver new blankets to Harry and Williamson as promised.

Our last stop is Rukanga to honor our commitment to the primary school. I want to show the children the video we filmed of their traditional dance. The teachers watch it first and are quite impressed. We show it on our computer screen and the children love it. They laugh and laugh, especially when their teacher is on the screen dancing. The rest of the children watch from the windows, so it's quite a spectacle. I ask to see the young girl who led the dance performers with perfect rhythm and cadence, all while calling out instructions in a melodic sing-song voice. Her name is Valley. I just want to acknowledge her for displaying such confidence in a predominantly boys' world.

When we arrive back on the coast, we treat ourselves with a visit to the Mtwapa Beach Hotel, a well-kept secret. We cozy up in the bar with our Maasai friends, have cokes, and laugh about all our travels together.

I pick up Moses's a-moody stick and begin twirling it like a baton. I remember more and more moves from my majorette days, and the place is in stitches. I even toss it into the air and am able to catch it and keep twirling. This starts a competition, and the baton is passed around to all who are gathered here. It is the beginning of the a-moody twirl.

The Ocean Cried

*Across the plain the long grass runs, before the
blowing weather, in loneliness the plain, the wind, the
heart, play together.*

—Karen Blixen

August 2004
Vipingo, Kenya

T he year in Kenya is coming to a close. How easy it
would be for me to remain here in the life I've created.
Africa has lured me in with its hauntingly beautiful landscapes, its astonishing wildlife, its friendliness with time,
but most of all with its residents who express gratitude for
the smallest of pleasures and good fortune.

I've lived within its political environment, refusing
to compromise my own values and yet gaining an understanding of how and why the citizens need to work within
the system to get their needs met. Learning of tribal traditions and ceremonies like branding the cheeks of the
Maasai babies, circumcising teenage girls to make them
marriageable, and removing the heads of dead skeletons to
honor the ancestors left me reeling at times, but in the end,

I didn't judge the people for their beliefs but congratulated them on their achievements and milestones.

Now, with sorrow in my heart, I leave our dear friends behind to continue their struggle for a unified Africa, a dream they can accomplish in their own time and season. My main hope is that I've made even a small difference in someone's life here, for they have made a huge difference in mine.

Back in Vipingo, Aaron and I are busy and stressed. We're packing for the trip back to the U.S. I'm making sure we have Kasi's vaccination record, certificate of good health, and her movement permit for immigration. The city kitty is going to America. She has more travel books to write.

I wonder if Aaron is still planning to buy this property from Mrs. Jonas, so I ask him.

"No," he shouts.

"Have you told Mrs. Jonas?"

"No."

"Don't you think you need to tell her? She is counting on you, and we are leaving tomorrow."

"Just fuck off! This is none of your business."

I want to run away. I head down to the small isolated beach off to the side of our oceanfront property and out of view of the rest of world.

Zachariah, having heard the conversation, is not far behind me. I welcome his companionship. We sit silently side by side in the warm sand. I feel like we are suspended in time on a deserted island. Zachariah and I have been spending a considerable amount of time together, running errands in town and videotaping his stories. I'm going to miss him terribly. I draw a tick tac toe game in the sand and we begin to play. When he tries to block me, I reach for his hand and notice how beautiful the contrast of brown and white looks together. He tells me about a dream he had a couple of nights ago, a dream of making love to me. His smile is radiant and contagious as he speaks. I have not thought of him romantically, but I do remember the day he came walking down the hall only wearing shorts. Maasai usually keep their bodies covered in my presence. I was able to see his muscular body and didn't mind taking a second glance as he passed by quietly.

He pleads with me to make love. He kisses my shoulder gently and continues down my arm, then brings my hands to his soft, full lips. I'm tempted. He holds my face and presses my cheek to his. I'm aroused. He kisses my neck and moves down my body. Just when I think I might be able to resist, he moves to my inner thighs. I can see his hardness through the thin shuka. "I don't know," I whisper.

He says, "Please, be free with me and I will be free with you."

I pull my dress up higher.

He whispers, "Are you ready?"

"Yes."

He gently slides his body on top of mine. I pull him closer and welcome him. We blend together. The orgasm I experience can only be described as primal, a complete re-lease physically and emotionally. It steals my breath and holds me captive for some time. I have totally let my guard down and given in to the moment.

I could stay here forever, but reality sets in, and I feel the obligation to get back to the house. I reach over and kiss Zachariah on both cheeks where tribal scars were placed with a hot iron when he was a baby. I plant a deep kiss on his willing lips. It makes me want to lie down and receive him again.

I head back to the house on shaky legs with my head spinning.

When I get close to the back door, I hear Aaron scream-ing, "God damn it!"

I cautiously open the door and see him jumping all over the place. He's obviously in some sort of pain.

I sheepishly ask, "What's going on?"

"I was putting on my shoes to come and find you when a scorpion bit me."

Moses and Katoo are searching out the errant creature. They locate it and remove it from our living space, Aaron says, "I believe this has been karma at work since I was rude and inconsiderate of your feelings earlier."

I spend the rest of the evening caring for him since he will be in pain for the next twelve hours. I place hot tow-els on his foot, bring him a painkiller with hot tea, prepare his favorite meal, and sit with him until he's able to fall asleep.

Even so, Zachariah occupies my thoughts. I didn't plan our romantic rendezvous, but it has left me dazed. I've always considered myself monogamous, but now I'm not sure what is happening. Granted, I'm not engaged or married, but if I'm sleeping with someone, in my mind, I'm in a committed relationship.

The next morning, as Zachariah and I pass each other in the hallway, we glance up briefly and then continue on with our heads lowered. Aaron walks down to see Mrs. Jonas as I finish packing. At the end of the day, Aaron and I head to the Nyali Beach Hotel. The guys leave quietly in another direction. We lock eyes and nod our upspoken goodbyes.

Early in the morning, we receive a call from the reception desk telling us there is a Maasai man at the gate requesting admittance to visit us. I run down the long steps through the gardens of jasmine flowers, breathing in my favorite fragrance. Happiness sweeps me away when I see Zachariah standing there. I felt a close connection with him before but didn't realize the depth of it until he brought it out in the light. We walk in silence along the beach of the Indian Ocean as the waves gently wash over our bare feet. In the stillness of the morning as the sun rises, we wade deeper into the turquoise waters.

When the sky sprinkles us with a light blessing, Zachariah holds his blanket over our heads as we spring to shore. "I consider you to be my wife," he says.

I realize I've surrendered much of my heart and soul to him and his Africa. Aaron catches up with us when it's almost time to head to the airport. I want to kiss Zachariah, but I hug him quickly instead. He places a giraffe necklace in my hand and whispers, "Please don't forget me." I cover his hand in shared respect. This is our final goodbye.

While flying from Mombasa to Nairobi, I can't hold back the tears. I will miss the days spent in the bush, laughing with Jasmine and Tempest while doing our daily chores, playing rummy with Aaron every night under candlelight, seeing fires on the horizon and praying for rain with the villagers in the dry season, and watching the vibrant sunsets spreading out over the plains toward Mt. Kenya. I will also miss living in Voi Town, connecting with Maasai warriors and their families, traveling to and fro on a whim in the Land Cruiser, and working for conservation in the Tsavo area.

I will remember best living the last three months on the coast, feeling the humid salty air on my skin, walking through the tide pools searching for obscure sea life, learning Maasai ways with my best friends, teaching classes to safari guides, all nurturing my connection with Africa.

But at this moment, I miss Zachariah most and wonder if it would be possible to just forget the world and be together regardless of time, space and differences in our cultures.

I call him from the airport, still teary-eyed, and tell him, "I cried on the plane all the way to Nairobi."

He responds passionately, "I will never forget our wonderful moment together and then our sorrowful good-bye. How painful in my heart. How lonely on my side." He pauses. "I cried and the ocean cried."

Part III

WHEN WIND AND WATER COLLIDE

Out beyond ideas of wrong doing and right doing, there is a field. I'll meet you there.

—Rumi, 13th century

Winds of War

*When I live my own life to the utmost; it is
easier to let others live theirs.*

—Courage to Change

Fall 2004
Sandpoint, Idaho

As our plane departs Jomo Kenyatta International Airport at sunset, I can make out a Maasai in traditional red herding his cattle down a dirt path. I watch until he slips out of sight.

The flight seems exceptionally long this time. And when we land in Detroit, I head in one direction to catch a flight to visit my family, while Aaron takes Kasigau, in the other direction, to be with his family.

A week with my family and friends is uplifting and gives me time to clear my head. When I land back in Idaho, I call Aaron to pick me up at the airport. His mother answers the phone and informs me that he won't be able to pick me up because he doesn't know what side of the road to drive on now that he is back in the U.S.

My blood feels like it is boiling. I say, "Thank you," and abruptly hang up.

I call Jessica and share my dilemma. I decide to splurge on a room for us at my favorite spa resort in Coeur d'Alene to celebrate my return. I don't tell Aaron or his mother my plan.

The next day we head back to the small town where we both live, and I spend the next few days with her. Aaron keeps calling, and I keep ignoring the calls. When I finally answer, he begs me to come home. I decide I will give this relationship a few months to recover and so, I rejoin him in the log cabin on his mother's property.

Back at work, I take the lead on a major project. It becomes my priority, and my relationship with Aaron takes a back seat. I work long, hard hours and give up my weekends. I'm so exhausted that at times I pull off to the side of the road to sleep when I'm headed into work. Aaron is not working, so he tries to take over some of the household duties. I still do all the cooking, and after dinner most nights, I either go back to my project planning or we watch TV.

I'm missing my life in Kenya and I'm trying to avoid decisions that I should be making here at home. The program I'm planning for the government should be outstanding. That is one thing that I'm sure of based on my dedication to replicating an event that happened years earlier. We will be celebrating Albeni Falls Dam's Fiftieth Anniversary. I have done research at the local library, copied all the related articles written back then, and studied all the files at the U.S.

Army Corps of Engineers Seattle District. The highlight of the celebration will be a flyover and fireworks just as it was done fifty years ago.

I'm also dealing with guilt since arriving home. This guilt has everything to do with returning to my life of opportunity and privilege and leaving my Kenyan friends behind with little hope of immediately improving their lives. I know Zachariah is grateful for his time working at the Ngulia Safari Lodge, a tourist hotel nestled high on a rugged overlook behind Kichwa Tembo, and I'm grateful they taught him English.

I can still picture the entrance gate to the Ngulia Rhino Sanctuary in Kenya's National Park System, with its large sheet-metal cutout of a rhinoceros. I affectionately remember a safari there with Aaron and Zachariah where I suggested we all channel leopards. A few minutes later, a leopard appeared from behind a rock formation in the middle of the day. The leopard glanced at us and then rushed into the bushes where he watched us intently.

Aaron and I have been together for almost three years. When I try to reminisce about Africa with him one day, he bluntly says, "That part of my life is over."

Aaron and I continue living together, but we quietly grow apart. Before long I begin creating a space for myself in the loft area of the log cabin we share. Virginia Wolfe said, *A woman must have money and a room of her own...* I now have money, but a room of my own, a place of retreat, is exactly what I need. I add all my favorite furniture, including a wicker chair with matching footstool, a room-size faux zebra rug, and accessories like the blessed prayer scarf I treasure from Nepal. When I need to overcome feelings of oxygen deprivation, I say to Aaron, "Tonight I'm going to sleep upstairs."

More often than not, Aaron will respond, "Oh, okay, I will come with you."

Not wanting to hurt his feelings, I just smile and he joins me.

But when I ask him to join me on a safari to Rwanda to finally see the mountain gorillas, once again, he declines.

Respite with Gentle Giants

What you do makes a difference, and you have to decide what kind of difference you want to make.

—Jane Goodall

Winter 2005
Virunga Mountains, Rwanda

Jessica agrees to go to Rwanda with me, and suggests we go to meet Jane Goodall at Washington State University before our departure. WSU is participating in ChimpanZoo, Jane's international research program dedicated to the study of captive chimpanzees to learn more about their behaviors and needs in captivity. We are given a tour of the research facility and have a chance to meet the resident chimps. Jane is also promoting her latest book, *The Chimpanzees I Love, Saving their World and Ours*. I'm thrilled and honored to be able to discuss the Roots & Shoots Youth programs with her. She's so engaging and continues to inspire me by the way she lives her life. I can still hear her soft-spoken but unyielding voice sharing, "Just follow your heart."

On the day of our trip departure, Aaron kisses me lightly on the cheek and whispers, "*Safari jema.*"

I thank him and am quickly off to catch my flight. Jessica wants to stop in London to sightsee for a couple of days, and I agree, even though I would not have chosen this stop. To my dismay, London is freezing, and the bed and breakfast we rent doesn't have central heating. After shivering in bed all night in the drafty room, I look forward to a hot gourmet breakfast. But we're served cold cereal. The only redeeming quality is Kenyan coffee served by our hostess, who is housesitting. She is from Africa and we immediately have a connection. The coffee and the interesting conversation warms me briefly.

Jessica and I do all the normal tourist things, like watching the Changing of the Guard, entering London Bridge, viewing Big Ben, and riding on the giant Ferris wheel, all in freezing temperatures with snowflakes falling. I'm miserable. I need to get to Africa and feel the warmth of the sun on my body.

Arrival in Nairobi is amazing. The high temperature thaws the memories of those cold gray days in London. We start out by revisiting my old hangouts and getting reacquainted with my wonderful Kenyan friends.

I begin a search to find Zachariah, but I'm not sure where he is or how I might get in touch with him. While in Nairobi, we stay at the Norfolk Hotel, and every night I have the pleasure of spending time with acquaintances old and new. But I know I'm going to have to get to Voi if I want to see my Maasai friends.

I call Steve Turner, and one of his guides, a Maasai, gives us a lift in an Origins Safaris Land Rover. When we're almost to Voi, we pass Weldon in a Land Cruiser. He recognizes me and comes to a quick stop. I jump in with him for the remainder of the trip to town.

Weldon has been in contact with Zachariah, and the next thing I know he's dialing his number and hands me the phone.

"Zachariah, is that you?"

"It's so good to hear your voice," he says.

"I have missed you so much," I add. "I'm in Voi town. Where are you?"

"I'm in the bush, but I can be in Voi by midnight."

"I can't wait to see you. You will find me at the Voi Wildlife Lodge. I will wait for you in the Gazebo Bar." My mind and body are filled with great anticipation and high expectations.

At the VWL, the resort manager introduces Jessica and me to former President Moi's daughter, who is also staying at the resort. She is friendly, and we enjoy having drinks and conversing. She insists that when we get to Kigali, Rwanda, we must see the orphaned Tutsi dancers. I make a mental note.

After a late dinner, I patiently wait alone for Zachariah. He arrives around midnight as predicted. I'm afraid our reunion will be awkward, but when he arrives, we immediately embrace. We sit in one of the overstuffed loveseats that I had come to cherish. We hold hands and marvel at the fact that we are together again. To add to our delight, a pair of young elephants are playing in the watering hole. We can barely see them in the scant moonlight, but think one is a male and the other a female displaying courtship behaviors.

Around 1:00 a.m., the elephants take leave, and that is our cue. Thankfully, the security guards on the property turn their heads as I sneak Zachariah past them to my room. I fumble with the key, enter, close the door, and directly pull Zachariah down on the bed. He caresses my face, neck, and shoulders. We kiss with a kind of passion I've never experienced. I want him desperately. I remove his belt but take the time to admire his muscular body before climbing on top and uniting us as one.

He comes immediately and with that explosion of passion, I experience another incredible orgasm, one that leaves me reeling. His smile lets me know how much he is enjoying my reaction. We make love again and again into the wee morning hours. The Maasai believe that when a woman has sex with a younger man, she becomes younger and more beautiful. I'm not sure if this is true, but I definitely feel younger.

Over breakfast, I tell Zachariah that I need to leave in an hour's time. I'm scheduled to fly to Kigali, Rwanda, and climb some of the highest peaks in the Volcanoes National Park in hopes of catching a glimpse of the threatened mountain gorillas, the groups habituated by Dian Fossey. Saying goodbye again is painful. We agree to figure out a way to stay in touch. I write my home address, phone number, and email on a VWL brochure and leave him once again.

Gorillas have been on my list since the early nineties. But in 1994, there was vague news coming from Kigali, the capital of Rwanda, of a tribal/ethnic war going on in this small country that is landlocked by Uganda, Tanzania, Burundi, and the Democratic Republic of the Congo. Later reports were very clear: the Hutu rebels killed over nine hundred thousand Tutsi, mainly with machetes. It was genocide of great proportions that lasted for one hundred days.

In 1999, as I was making final arrangements for a trip to the Virunga Mountains in Rwanda, I heard of an American couple who had been killed while trekking to see the rare gorillas.

(AP) 8 Tourists Slain in Uganda, Including U.S. Couple Treks through the Bwindi Impenetrable Forest of Uganda to see rare mountain gorillas are exclusive forays that begin in a tranquil agricultural valley. That calm was shattered on Monday when eight tourists, including an American couple, were hacked or bludgeoned to death in the forest by a band of rebels armed with automatic rifles, machetes and spears who were said to be remnants of ethnic Hutu militias that carried out mass kill-ings in Rwanda in 1994.

For a time, I let go of the dream. Then in 2003, Rwan-da began its struggle to foster ethnic reconciliation and

political stability. Despite the problems, the country managed to stabilize the environment for its endangered mountain gorillas, and a small but growing ecotourism industry
centered on the animals was developing.

Aaron and I were living in Kenya during this time and I
remembered the gorillas. That's when I asked Steve Turner
if we could trade our car for a trip to Rwanda before our year
came to an end. Steve didn't take the deal because our car
wasn't a good fit for his safari fleet, and Aaron refused to
work with me to make our own arrangements.

Six years later, I'm finally on my way. When Jessica and I
reach Kigali, I insist our guide take us to see the Tutsi dancers and drummers, an incredibly talented group of young-
sters. I'm so glad we made this detour. Then in the bank in
Rungheri, the small town at the foot of the Virunga Hills, a
bank teller shares some compelling information about the
gorilla twins that were born on the mountain four months
ago. He encourages us to see them since they are the only
twins to survive in the gorilla population.

We have arrived during the long rains, and our accommodations are sparse to say the least. So what does this
mean for us? Wet clothing that won't dry, damp bedding, a
dripping shower with cold water, wet towels to dry off with,
and cold food. The climbs are tough through the dense rain
forest but are worth the struggles. We spend much of our
time on hands and knees crawling through the underbrush,
and our fingers take the brunt of the stinging nettles. If we
do encounter our assigned group, we will only have one

hour to observe and photograph. If the group becomes upset, we will be forced to leave.

Journal Entry: Incredible Day

Arise at 3:00 am –Coffee at 4:00 a.m. – Depart at 4:30 am – Arrive Park HQ at 6:30 am

Groups are forming: only four groups with ten persons in each, maximum allowed on the mountain per day. Photographer Joseph Brown has his own group of eight and they are climbing to the highest point to see the twins. Jessica and I volunteer to join them. The look on his face gives away his dismay. I suspect that he's concerned because this is our first day on the mountain and he thinks that we will hold up his group.

We drive to the mountains. It is 7:00 am and we arrive at 9:00 am. I attach myself to our Rwandan leader, Francis. I match him step for step as we climb to 10,000 ft. to our group of gorillas at 9,600 ft.

I'm told that we have climbed above the group and view from there so that we don't cause them to climb higher. It works. The silverback of our gorilla group accepts us reluctantly and we not only catch a glimpse of our subjects, we sit right next to these magnificent creatures and look into their sympathetic eyes. The twins are delightful as they tumble over one another rolling down the hill. A teenage gorilla wants to join in the fun but the mom strikes the juvenile, who whines away dejected. Our hour is over so soon and then it's time to leave the group behind and trudge down the mountain. Children, young entrepreneurs, engage with us along the trail selling their drawings of the gorillas. They are great ambassadors for their country and I will proudly display their art when I get back home. The sun is shining down in the valley and we sit on the veranda of a cottage on a small lake. The owner provides peanut butter sandwiches for our lunch. I'm warm once again and happy to make a donation to the Dian Fossey Gorilla Fund International at www.gorillafund.org to support their efforts to continue to protect these majestic East African primates.

Before catching our flight to Nairobi, we visit the Kigali Memorial Center and walk through the Memorial Gardens where mass graves have been created for the bodies of the genocide. I can't help but cry when two bodies, discovered in a remote church basement, arrive today for proper burial. We are told that bodies continue to be found even over ten years later. It starts out as a sad day but brightens when we stop by the Hotel Des Mille Collines, site of the inspiring story of survival, during the genocide, portrayed in the movie, *Hotel Rwanda.*

Back in Nairobi we have dinner with Steve Turner. He is planning to lead a group to document a Samburu Circumcision Ceremony with a side trip down the Omo River in Ethiopia. He invites me to join him. I immediately accept. All I can think about is another trip to Africa on the horizon.

Fight or Flight

*You ask your heart if you should stay or leave. If you
are meant to leave, you will be shown the path.*

—Anne Morrow Lindbergh

*Spring 2005
Sandpoint, Idaho*

Upon my return Aaron has resumed helping his mother run the family tree farm. He also works on projects for me. He is trying to restore my Jeep Wrangler to its original condition and has started building a small writer's retreat down by the lake so that I will be inspired to work on the book. I'm appreciative, but something is just not clicking for me. I believe the unrest I'm feeling has to do with the fact that I want to travel again and Aaron seems content to stay put.

I know that Aaron is sensing my withdrawal from our connection. He tries to engage me in conversation when I return from work each day, but I have shut down emotionally. One day when I come home late from a trying day, he is sitting in front of the fireplace and asks me to join him. He has cinnamon spice tea, my favorite, ready for me. I take a sip, then relax with a deep sigh. The fire is crackling with sparks, the kind of sparks that I would like to feel once again with Aaron.

He looks into my eyes and speaks in earnest. "Are you willing to make a long-term commitment to me?"

I'm stunned by this impulsive request but more so by the response that flies unfettered out of my mouth. "I'm just here one day at a time."

"So then why are you here at all?"

All the muscles in my body constrict. I can't speak.

He jumps up, moves over to his desk, and sweeps his favorite giraffe wood carving from the Norfolk Hotel onto the floor. I quickly take refuge in the loft. Staying in a situation with any kind of conflict is scary for me. As a child, I was frozen in fear when my parents fought. It was usually late at night when I was already in bed, but in our small house I heard every cruel and hurtful word. Most of the arguments involved my mother accusing my father of being with other women, something that I did not fully understand. I became so distraught once during an extremely violent episode, I started vomiting. I continued through the next day and the next until I was throwing up green bile. That was the day my mother invited the Baptist minister to our house for counseling since my father had stopped coming home. This did not go well, and not long after, I called my mother to my bedside. "Please get Daddy to come home. I want to see him before I die."

Mom ran to the neighbor's house for help. We had not been able to seek assistance from doctors in the past because my father believed that nature, not medical professionals, provided the answers to overcome illnesses. We ate healthy foods, mainly from our garden, exercised regularly, slept with the windows open even during the winter months in Ohio, and did not visit doctors or take medications or supplements. I perceived that my father saw any illness as a sign of weakness; therefore, I needed to be strong at all times. The neighbor came to my aid and called her doctor for a prescription. In a few days I recovered, but I made a vow that I would never let them hurt me like that again.

I believe there is a side of Aaron that has been simmering on the burner ready to boil over. I glance out the window and sit in the silence of a magnificent sunset, its vivid orange-red hues turning to pink then purple.

Eight months after our return from Kenya, I leave Aaron the only way I know how; the way my father left me. I kiss Aaron and even pull him back into bed before he heads out to a seminar to find another healer. I visualized this moment, when I would see him off and then be free to leave without a word of goodbye.

Traveling with a lover can present each person in a new, brighter light or reveal flaws of character. I can say that I saw Aaron, at times, in a new, brighter light, but I struggled with his lack of concern about following through on promises that were made to our Kenyan friends. I tried to live up to those promises for him. I believed that whatever he promised and then didn't do was a reflection on my character.

As soon as he pulls out of the driveway, I call Jessica. We load all my personal belongings into a small U-Haul trailer in preparation to drive down that long winding gravel driveway to the main highway for the very last time. The only item I leave behind is the buffalo-hide shield that hangs high up on a beam of the A-frame log cabin. I can still see Maasai Moses holding his spear in one hand and the shield in the other. I carry with me the ostrich-feather headdress that Maasai Zachariah presented to me as a going-away gift. Now I realize how much I miss that life. What I need is time and space where no one can contact me and I can sort out my life. I lock the door and slip the key underneath the doormat.

I did not want to model my parents' relationship and cast hurtful words at one another like stones. I really wanted things between Aaron and me to be like they were when we first met, but in "The Ballad of Reading Gaol" by Oscar Wilde it says:

Each man kills the thing he loves,
By each let this be heard,
Some do it with a bitter look,
Some with a flattering word,
The coward does it with a kiss,
The brave man with a sword!
I am the coward.

Later I will learn that as Aaron was driving home from his seminar, he had stopped for a red light when the sudden thought that I had left him popped into his head. When he arrived at the log house, he realized it was true. He climbed back in the car and went searching for me all the way to the Montana border. He couldn't understand why I'd abandoned him, especially since I had pulled him back into bed earlier in the morning. He tried to reach me, but I had turned off my cell phone and left it off for the next few days. It would be some time before he would receive an explanation, a painful period for him, but I had moved on and would soon be facing danger in Lake Turkana.

Riding Out the Storm

*The past has flown away. The coming month and year
do not exist. Ours only is the present's tiny point.*

—Mahmud Shabistari

Summer 2005
Omo River Delta/Lake Turkana, Kenya

Someone's arms are wrapped around my waist, another's around my legs.

Someone is yelling, "Are you okay?"

There is no time to respond.

I just nod as I hear Thaddeus's panicked voice. "Bail faster!"

Larry and Steve are bailing with coffee mugs and water bottles; I use my hands. The gasoline containers are drifting farther and farther from us. After several tense moments, the changing winds drive us in another direction, and Thaddeus decides to steer us towards a small, rocky landmass. We head to a small inlet, but as we approach, the howling wind drives us back out to sea. After several attempts, Thaddeus successfully brings us to shore. I swiftly jump out, ecstatic to have my feet on solid ground.

Thaddeus, exhausted but laughing, says, "We were minutes away from having to toss your bags and cameras into the sea."

We laugh too, because now we're safe; at least, for the moment. As we acclimate ourselves to this place of sanctuary, we have another cause for concern. This isle in the desert sea is called North Island and is notorious for its poisonous snakes. But some Native fisherman have also taken refuge here and assure us that all the snakes are gone.

I'm overdue for a pit stop. This is an edgy proposition. I contemplate whether I would prefer to scout for crocodiles hidden in the weeds, as I did along the riverbanks of the Omo River for the past nine days, or watch out for snakes lurking behind the rocks farther from shore. I venture out towards an overhang and find a large rock to squat behind.

Drying out all our belongings is first; lunch is next on the agenda. Thaddeus joins me as we feast on soggy sandwiches. Steve has told him about my year in Kenya, and he wants to hear all about my experience living in the bush. He is fascinated. When the errant winds subside a couple hours later, we reluctantly climb back into the boat. First, we search and recover the gas containers. Then we motor to the east side of the lake, where we will meet the Leakey's at their Research Center.

Famed paleoanthropologist Dr. Richard Leakey and his wife, Meave, daughter, Louise, and their colleagues work in this arid northern region of Kenya's Turkana Basin, also called the Cradle of Mankind, to unravel the mysteries of human evolution. The area is known as *Koobi Fora* in the language of the nearby Gabbra people. The name means "a place of the source of myrrh," a common plant in this area.

We hear the roar of a Cessna 206, the bush plane of Africa, and see the Leakeys waving to us from the sky. They are departing for Nairobi to speak at a national symposium. We missed our meeting time by over three hours.

Another bush plane is coming in for a landing. It's Edwin, our pilot. Leaving the lake and the boat behind is a blessing. We thank Thaddeus for his extraordinary boating skills. I'm unaware that I'll have another chance meeting with Thaddeus, but it's no surprise that the universe already has a plan in place. We spend an evening together at the Oasis Lodge in 2009 when I return and promise to stay in touch and see one another again. Not long after our evening at the Oasis, I received a message from Steve Turner, saying, "Thaddeus was killed in a head-on crash, riding on his motorcycle, dodging oncoming traffic in Nairobi." The news saddened me.

Today we're bouncing down the dirt runway of Koobi Fora as we continue south along the eastern edge of Lake Turkana onto the Desert Rose Lodge. Hot winds blow.

The wood and stone lodge features great views of Mt. Nyiru, the spiritual mountain of the Samburu. I can even see the mountain from my walled, open-air garden shower, which is tiled in tiny mosaics of the desert rose flower.

The proprietors of this secluded haven are a nice young Italian couple who have two small children. They have taken in a young woman from India whose American husband divorced her and sent her home. Since she is no longer considered marriageable in her native land, she has come here and works as a massage therapist.

But the reason we're here and what I've been waiting for is the Samburu Circumcision Ceremony that Steve has invited us to record. This ceremony might be the last for this nomadic tribe that's being forced to abandon its cultural heritage.

I'm especially excited because of my connection with the Maasai tribe. The Samburu are technically cousins of the Maasai, the same Maa language and Maa traditions but subtle differences in the color of beads and fabrics worn.

Zachariah, my Maasai confidant, taught me many things about his tribe, but I especially appreciated his telling of the Maa ceremonies and rituals. Zachariah and I also discussed female circumcision, which is practiced by the Maasai and Samburu. He insisted that the girls want to have this done and that the purpose is for cleanliness as it is for the boys, but I don't believe that for one minute. Some man thought this up and put it into practice to keep the females from wandering off and finding lovers. A girl cannot be married until she's circumcised, so of course, she wants to have it done.

I n Mtwapa, the coastal town on the Indian Ocean near Vipingo where Aaron and I lived during our last three months in Kenya, the Samburu would congregate on one side of the main street and the Maasai on the other. Both groups would wave to us, but Moses, our Maasai friend, who resided with us, would always laugh at the Samburu warriors wearing plastic flowers as a part of their headdresses.

Once, as he and I shopped at the market, we saw a young man of European descent dressed as a Samburu warrior. Moses was doubled over shaking from hilarity. I was also doubled over in reaction to his amusement.

In the months that followed, as I was tearfully planning my return to the U.S., Moses would grin and say, "White Samburu." Then he would explode with laughter, infecting me once again. Sadly, a few years later, Moses was mistaken for a thief and beaten up by the local police. He was put in jail, a place where, it is said, the Maasai die because they cannot see beyond the existing moment. Moses was eventually taken to a hospital in Oloitokitok where he passed away, too broken, physically and emotionally, to be fixed.

*

T he Desert Rose Lodge provides an evening for de-compressing. Tomorrow at sunrise the circumcision ceremony begins, but tonight we congregate outside on the wood deck in the shade of Mt. Nyrui. We luxuriate in a fabulous six-course dinner served on fine china at tables draped with crisp white tablecloths. Each table features a centerpiece arranged with the local flower, the desert rose, and pink candles complete the arrangement. What a contrast to our days on the Omo River.

Honoring Ancient Traditions

In the face of some Maasai matriarchs could be read the tale of a people whose iron code of tradition makes them unique among the earth's beings.

—Robert Vaira, from "A Tent with a View"

Summer 2005
Samburu Village, Kenya

I n Maasai society, circumcision is a ritual that signifies the passing of childhood. This ceremony is celebrated every ten years or so and always on the full moon or new moon. Once boys have been circumcised, they graduate to become Moran, new recruits to the rank of warrior. The ceremony establishes the first age-set in Maasai society. The ceremony has to be planned at least two months in advance. Honey beer is prepared, and the elders arrive to witness the event. The boys, from twelve to twenty years of age, dress in black aprons, and are decorated with white chalk. A couple of days ago they climbed high up into the mountains to collect resin from the trees to be used in another part of the ritual.

We can actually hear leopards in the morning as we prepare to move to the circumcision village. Acacia thorn branches block entrance to the manyatta. We won't be invited to see the actual cutting, but we hear the chanting and are told that each boy will sit on a goatskin in front of his mother's manyatta. Fresh milk will be sprinkled on his private parts as the circumciser approaches with the knife. Young men who flinch or even blink will dishonor their families. We sit with a family, converse, and see the boys in their black aprons awaiting the ceremony. They have serious faces. All is ready now for the blessings to begin. Men come to bless the papas, and women to bless the mamas.

It is first light of the full moon. The traveling circumciser, who we met yesterday, comes by us. The elders gather round each boy. The circumciser moves quickly with the knife. The boy is then carried into the house and put upon a bed. A bull cow will be bled later in the day, and the boy will consume a mixture of blood, tea, and milk for the next four days.

I think about the Maasai women I met and know that they have endured female circumcision with the same honor and dignity as they reached womanhood. I have been told that the girls dress in black and wear distinctive headdresses decorated with cowrie shells to symbolize fertility. During their six-week recovery period, the young women are not permitted to talk to men or strangers. Long beaded tassels or chains hang from their headdresses and partially cover their faces to demonstrate this exclusion. After completing this initiation, Maasai women are allowed to marry.

I miss my Maasai friends, especially Zachariah. He has kept in touch by having someone write letters to me. I savor those words. Now I'm glad to have Henri, a Maasai guide, with us for this part of the trip. I ask him if he knows Zachariah, but he doesn't. I'm disappointed.

Our Samburu guide, Alex, stays with Elizabeth and me throughout the day. Alex asks me to take a picture of him with his two brothers who have just been circumcised. He also asks for pain relievers for them. I'm shocked and surprised by this, but in the afternoon, I go to the lodge and return with two extra-strength Tylenol capsules.

Stan arrives just as I see a Samburu elder with two spears. A young warrior arrives to interpret. The elder is anxious to sell me a spear given to him by his father when he was a boy. I begin to negotiate for their purchase, and Stan indicates that he would like one. We negotiate together and make a deal for 1600 ksh. The elder asks a moran to count it for him. He is happy, and Stan and I run back to the lodge with our spears held high over our heads as if we are warriors.

When we return to the village, a dance has begun. I'm delighted, since I have made a commitment to dance in every country I travel through. I believe we are all dancing through life instinctively in our own special way and the music today is uplifting.

The villagers congregate in the center of the village, and a few cows are brought in. Alex tries to protect me from the bulls that must know what is about to happen, for they are stomping, kicking, and trying to run off. I witness the bleeding of a bull right in front of me. I'm told that this won't be painful for the animal and will not kill it.

The bull is pure white, a requirement for this special occasion. One young man is holding the mouth and an ear, another is holding its tail, and a third is aiming with a bow and arrow to the jugular vein. I'm hoping that this will go quickly, but it doesn't. It takes several punches to penetrate the artery, and once that happens, blood spurts out of an angry vessel and lands in a pool near my feet. A woman runs up with a large gourd and catches the remaining blood. I follow her into the manyatta where she stirs it with a stick to get the blood to clot. This is mixed with milk and tea and heated. Her son is already sitting up in bed and ready to drink the concoction. I remember a similar time when a Maasai woman gave birth. A goat was slaughtered and its blood mixed with milk into a soup the woman would drink for the next four days.

As the sun sets, I start walking back. A Samburu woman stops me. She is matronly, past childbearing age perhaps, head shaved like all married women here, muscular and stern. I smile and then she breaks into giggles. She holds up a light brown gourd. It's beautiful and artfully decorated. I offer her 200 ksh, and she is happy to hand the piece to me. Henri tells me it was used during the blessings today. It still has some butter in it that the elders placed on the heads of the fathers.

It's interesting how people come into my life especially when I'm moving about on my own and living in the moment. Back at the lodge, I sit in front of the fireplace where the burning wood crackles softly. Stan and Larry ask, "Please tell us all about your year living in Kenya." We chat late into the night.

We take two vehicles out in the morning to see the boys gathering bird feathers for their headdresses. They use a bow and arrows with a gum resin so they just stun the bird without destroying it. The feathers are hung from the headdress and give the appearance of birds that are still alive. This seems to be a competition for the young men with the purpose of securing their rank in the tribe. Some take this seriously while others act like normal teenagers and find it a time to joke and have some fun. They are playfully teasing us and love posing for photos.

For several months after the ceremony, the circumcised boys will continue to dress in black, paint their faces white, and wear bird feather headdresses that indicate their status.

The Samburu are grateful for our presence and our ability to share their story with the rest of the world. I have come to realize that the practice of gratitude is at the root of most indigenous traditions.

To honor and thank the guests, a goat is slaughtered and grilled for our dinner, including the Samburu tradition of offering the guests its blood. I enjoy the grilled goat meat but leave the blood for others to partake. We say good night and goodbye to the villagers, for we are planning an early departure. As I close my eyes, I hear a leopard's rasping voice in the distance. It's hard to imagine what adventure might be coming next, but I'm ready to submit to the *will of the winds.*

Embracing the Moment

As long as you live,
keep learning how to live...

—Seneca, Native American tribe

Summer 2005
Lake Turkana, Kenya

R ain awakens me, and I'm not ready to leave behind the
comforts of the Desert Rose Lodge. I'll miss the candlelight dinners outside in the Nyrui Mountains, the cool
air, and the crackling sound of the wood fires while enjoying good conversation over a nightcap.

Today we caravan across the Chalbi Desert to Mount
Marabit. I envision camel trains traversing through the
sandscape with date palms waving in the breeze at the oasis. Here we encounter the Rendille, Samburu, Turkana, and
El Molo tribes where they are said to live in harmony. When
we reach Lake Turkana, I run down through the rocks to the
shore to touch the water, warm and wonderful. It's time to
make peace with the lake gods, who already have future adventures in store for me.

I delight in spending every free moment in the warm mineral spring pool at the Oasis Lodge & Club on the southeastern shore in the town of Loiyangalani, "a place of many trees," in the native Samburu tongue. Wolfgang, a German expat, manages the lodge and hires locals to help run this basic establishment. I have a room to myself. A bar in the reception area attracts the likes of us. Scenes from *The Mountains of the Moon* and *The Constant Gardner* were filmed here. Mount Kulal is visible in the distance as we dine on the day's catch of fresh tilapia.

A Rendille tribal member invites us to attend a ceremonial dance this evening. By the time we arrive, the dance chant has already begun. I begin to dance and notice one small girl mimicking my moves and making strange facial expressions. Then it dawns on me that she is also mimicking my facial expressions. We laugh. As the dance chant picks up tempo, the small child pushes through the crowd and tugs on my skirt and won't let go. For days I have wanted to pick up and hold a small child but have never felt that it would be an acceptable gesture. Today I know the time is right, so I reach down and pick up this precious girl. She hugs me and we dance.

A young Kenyan man approaches and speaks in the king's English. "Her name is Diana. She is two years old."

Through McDonald, our interpreter/driver, I'm invited to spend much of the next two days with Diana. Her home is a grass and mud hut that houses her mother, brothers, and sisters, six in all. Drawings hang on the white-washed walls surrounding the benches and beds and a small table that make up the one-room house. McDonald listens intently and then shares with me, "Her father has died recently of unknown causes. She is part Rendille and part Samburu."

I learn that for several reasons most females don't have an opportunity to attend school. First, they are responsible for helping with household chores. Second, they tend the goats while their brothers attend school. And third, they're responsible for taking care of their grandmothers. Even if they have a chance to go to school, most girls will quit school when they reach menstruation age because of the stigma and a lack of feminine products. In some tribes, girls are sent to a special hut to stay during their menses.

I offer to adopt Diana in the sense that I will provide financial support for her schooling. The family is very happy. I'm happy because I might be able to make a difference in her life. I will continue to pay her annual school fees, approximately fifty dollars, and purchase her books and uniforms as long as she stays in school. I've made arrangements to stay in touch through the nearby Catholic mission. Saying goodbye to her for now is difficult but I plan to return one day.

We move on to the Kalacha Oasis and the Kalacha Community Lodge. This desert oasis sustains the Gabbra. These are people of the desert. Here we enjoy our last days in remote areas, with palm trees, clear blue skies, sunsets that last longer than usual, bright stars, and views of camel trains crossing the desert.

When our charter plane arrives from Nairobi, I'm not feeling well. An inflamed tooth has been bothering me for the past two days. I barely slept last night. I'm not looking forward to seeing a dentist in Nairobi. The doctor, maybe a dentist, says that I have an infection in the gum. Now I'm actually anxious to return home.

I've been thinking about Aaron and missing the fun-loving playful side of him. I miss the laughter and the companionship. I remember our first night in the bush, hitchhiking to Mombasa, sleeping in the manyatta during the Maasai wedding, and singing and bathing in the rain in Voi. I ponder the idea of reaching out to him when I get back to see if we might be able to be friends again like in the beginning. My feelings for Aaron and my feelings for Africa are still intertwined and need to be unraveled.

*

A aron tried in vain to reach me before I departed for Ethiopia. I avoided him, but now that I am back home, I hope he will take my call. He does. We meet on the pedestrian boardwalk over an inlet on Lake Pend Oreille. We stroll along the shore as we have done many times before. I apologize for the way I left him and suggest we try to salvage our friendship.

"I've missed you, Aaron. I want you to know that I faced a fight or flight situation that day. Choosing flight has become a pattern of mine. I have trouble addressing even the slightest disagreements. After burying my feelings, I can no longer see the light of day, and then the only way I can survive is to leave the way I left you that gloomy Saturday morning."

Aaron hugs me and says, "Yes, let's be friends." He suggests we have lunch at one of our favorite cafes, Spuds. I accept and the lines between friendship and relationship begin to blur straightaway as if I've walked into a swirling dust devil.

To celebrate our renewed friendship, we make a trip to the Canadian Rockies, where we bathe in the Mullenmoth Hot Springs, photograph an elk herd meandering down the main street of Banff, canoe on Lake Louise, shower under a glacier melt waterfall, and then make love in the high summer grass of Jasper. It all happens so fast. It's like falling in love for the first time all over again. The sparks are back.

Riding Off into the Sunset

*Many of our challenges with anger occur
when we choose between having a
relationship and having a self.*

—Harriet Lerner

Fall 2005
Gulfport, Mississippi

As Aaron and I navigate our new relationship, Hurricane Katrina hits the Gulf Coast. I volunteer for a three-month assignment with USACE and FEMA. Aaron thinks I'm abandoning him again but we promise to talk on the phone every day and we do. I'm hoping that our astrological signs of air and water mix well this time around.

When my assignment comes to an end in November, I rush to catch my flight and take my last glance as the late afternoon sunlight skims across the ocean, making it look as if giant diamonds are sparkling in renewal and hope. Only months before, washing machines, refrigerators, and all sorts of debris floated in these same waters. I'm especially happy to be going home knowing that the people in the Gulf are rebuilding their lives and glad I was able to be there to witness their resilience.

Landing in the northwest on a Saturday night feels perfect. I alert Aaron that I'll be in our small town by midnight.

"I'll be sleeping by then. How about we meet tomorrow at Spuds for lunch."

My gut tells me something is amiss, but I'm so tired that I don't want to think about it. As I drive the lonely road back to our town, I pass the entrance to Aaron's compound. I'm tempted to drive down that long gravel driveway back into his arms, but I'll wait for that reunion to happen tomorrow. I'm really happy to be heading back to my own place, where I warm myself by the fire, make a cup of tea, and sit in silence.

I wake early and a feeling of loneliness overcomes me. I find the sweater Aaron gave me for my birthday and put on my favorite corduroy pants. I apply make-up wanting to look my best in anticipation of seeing Aaron for the first time in nearly three months. I wonder if he's feeling the same excitement.

When I arrive for lunch, he's waiting outside.

"You look great," I gush as we hug. He smiles.

On the way in I notice Michael, Aaron's good friend, sitting by himself at a booth by the front door. I give him a friendly greeting but feel a tightening in my throat as I continue to follow the hostess as she leads Aaron and me to a booth by the back window overlooking the lake.

My favorite song, "Can't Help Falling in Love with You", is filling the room. My favorite soup, roasted squash, is the feature of the day. And here I am sitting across from the man I plan to spend the rest of my life with but his blue eyes that usually sparkle so brightly look dull today.

"I'm so happy to finally get to see you. I've imagined this reunion every day since I left for the Gulf."

All I need to complete this moment is to be held tight and told that everything is going to be all right. I realize I'm vulnerable and in a weak state of shock from what I've seen and heard during the recovery efforts on the coast.

As I begin to share my stories of the heroic people who have just been through the

the worst natural disaster in U.S. history, Aaron pulls legal-size documents from his briefcase.

"I had these prepared for us to sign to seal our business venture."

I'm thrown off balance. We had discussed a business plan to market my travel book and his wildlife photographs, but, for me, they were secondary to our personal plans.

"These are documents set up to protect us in case of illness or death, and it outlines our financial arrangements."

"Why now? We have plenty of time to discuss this."

"I also need to share something else with you." He looks sheepish and hesitates.

"Go ahead," I say, thinking that it will be something exciting. But without warning a cyclone is ready to engulf me.

"Well, I'm getting married."

"You're what?" I turn away, feeling like I'm caught in a riptide and being sucked to the bottom of the ocean. Seconds pass. I don't know how many. "You're not serious? You can't be serious!"

"Yes, I'm getting married."

A tidal wave of despair slaps me in the face. I want these words to wash away as if they were never spoken. More moments pass. And then the anger comes. "You've been planning this behind my back. How could you?" I don't even ask who he's marrying. I could care less at this moment. "Well, have a nice life." I say without looking at him.

"But what about our business plans?" he asks.

This time I do not have any trouble saying the words that evaded me a few months earlier. They come easily to me now. "Goodbye, Aaron."

Attempting to make a dignified exit after explicitly stating my final adieu, I awkwardly wriggle to free myself from the constraints of the cafe booth. I gather my belongings and stiffly throw my wrap over my shoulders in a defiant manner. Aaron nervously fumbles with the bill and he doesn't try to stop me. I have to pass Michael on my way out. He glances at me as I briskly round the corner, my heart racing, but as I get closer, he looks away as if he is embarrassed. I bet he knew all along what was about to go down.

Now I realize that Aaron and I had been on too many passionate quests to break apart gently, most recently our Canadian adventure. As our deep connection unravels, I'm forced to admit that the universe might be delivering a well-deserved karmic gift wrapped in 'what-goes around-comes-around.'

It's winter and I long for the hot, bright, sunny days of Kenya. I see depression as my enemy, not an old friend I can invite in for a cup of tea as a therapist suggests. Then an intervention of sorts presents itself, a chance to do another assignment in the Gulf as a public relations specialist.

Aaron hears that I will be leaving soon and asks to stop by with some items I left behind on my rush to leave him earlier in the year. I heard he met his new wife on the day I deserted him, the day he headed to Spokane for a seminar that she was also attending. They became friends, and when I went to Katrina, they became lovers.

Knowing this might be our last time together, I say, "You know, we could have had it all."

"Yes, I know." He pauses briefly. then adds, "I can't wait to meet you again in another life and find out what's really behind those incredible smiling eyes." He turns and walks away.

Soon thereafter, the NAI commissions me to write a cover story on my Omo River trip for *Legacy* magazine. I'm thrilled and happy to meet their terms. It'll be my first published cover story and will reach over ten thousand people in thirty-three countries. My new life as a writer/photographer emerges.

On my flight departing the Northwest, I reflect on the past few years.

With Aaron, I was a more courageous rendition of my-self, and I believe it was the same for him. We would not have embarked on such an amazing adventure without the love and support of the other. If there was a flaw in our re-lationship, it had to be our lack of communication. But what mattered most is that we said yes to adventure, to the un-known, to possibilities. *Thank you, Aaron.*

I have walked away from relationships in the past so that I might have a better relationship with myself. But in the way I left, at times, I inflicted the pain of abandonment onto others. For this I am truly sorry. Each one of us has the right to achieve our goals and dreams in life and that's my wish for everyone. Life is full of twists and turns, detours, and dead ends; therefore, I continue to ask myself these same questions: *Why am I here on this earth? What is my pur-pose? Am I on the right path?*

"Excuse me, ma'am. Would you like something to drink?" the flight attendant startles me.

The woman sitting next to me laughs.

"Oh, yes, I would like a Coke, please. Thank you."

My seatmate introduces herself, and we find we have much in common. She's also an international traveler who has just returned from a trip to Asia where she made stops in five countries.

My intrigue gets the best of me. "So how are you able to make so many stops?"

"Delta Airlines has an Around the World trip tick-et that's good for one year. I make this an annual event to visit new places as I attend my required conventions abroad."

"Really. How many countries can you go to?"

"You can have a maximum of ten stops. They must be moving in one direction, revolving either east to west or west to east."

"Interesting." This makes me think about what Virginia Woolf said, *"As a woman, I have no country. As a woman, I want no country. As a woman, my country is the whole world."* My experiences on the African continent made me realize how much I still have to learn about other cultures in faraway places.

We land, and as I'm thanking her for this exciting information, I find myself sketching a route on the globe in my head from east to west. As I prepare to depart the Northwest, I'm leaving a free, independent woman who's not afraid to travel the world alone. As a child my father always loved hearing me say, "I want to be the one to climb on the horse and ride off into the sunset." He would be so proud of me.

I decide I will purchase a ten-stop ticket to places with attention-grabbing names like Jakarta, Bali, Fiji Islands, Beijing, Bhutan, Tibet, Singapore, Casablanca, Cairo, and Jerusalem. A new country every month, a new adventure every day.

I will leave the details up in the air for a favorable wind to carry them along.

Acknowledgments

It's hard to imagine that there will never be another road trip with my favorite traveling companion, my mother, and it brings tears to my eyes. We will never again drive through Cades Cove with the windows down playing Andrea Bocelli's *Time to Say Goodbye* serenading the deer that were grazing out in the open meadow, plus a lifetime supply of banter and snacks between us traversing the continental United States into Canada and Mexico. *Thank you, Mom.*

Dad was my hero who was always encouraging me to discover, explore, and experience all of life. His motto – we have places to go, things to do, and people to meet. Even though my father never left the continental United States, he always found places for us to go, things for us to do, and most importantly, people for us to meet. *Thank you, Dad.*

Love to my awesome sons, Douglas and Derek. You guys navigated through your lives with grace and understanding beyond your years. I'm so proud of you.

To my loving family and friends who have supported my effort to complete this book. I am grateful for your desire to see me reach this worthy endeavor. *Thanks!*

Thank you to literary agent, Lisa Hagan, for believing that I have a story worth telling and honoring my burning desire to inspire others to embrace our diversity while celebrating our oneness and to Inna Savchuk for designing an impressive book cover representing the book's title.

And to all the fearless females that came before me. You have been my inspiration to take risks, go beyond boundaries, and never stop exploring. *Thank you for sharing your stories.*

A *special thank you* to my amazing team: Jennifer Chesak, Wandering in the Words, for your developmental editing, to Barbara Biehler, Cindy McCain, Melissa Davie, Rebecca West, Sheyla Paz Hicks, Edith Constanza, Bridgette Rooks, Paula Munier, and Lisa Malone for volunteering to read the manuscript, make comments and do edits, to Tim Merriman, Lisa Brochu, and Paul Caputo from the National Association of Interpretation (NAI) for publishing my short travel stories in Legacy magazine, to members of the Zeitgeist writers' group for providing your invaluable critiques of my work, to Corey Gonzales for promotion on his podcast, and last, but not least, to Mark Mingrone, my webmaster, for designing the perfect webpage *deeflower. com.*

About the Author

D ee Flower has travelled to over 40 countries on six continents. Her career as a park ranger sparked her love of adventure. On a safari with The National Association of Interpreters (NAI) she fell in love with Africa and has lived with the Taita and Maasai tribes while documenting their oral histories. Her cover story "Rural Africa" was featured in *Legacy* magazine in 2006. When not travelling, exhibiting her photos, or fulfilling speaking engagements, she assists individuals with disabilities find enriching employment in the community. Dee is a graduate of Kent State University and resides in Nashville, Tennessee.

Made in the USA
Monee, IL
25 September 2022